W9-AUI-832

# QUICK FROM SCRATCH
# HERBS & SPICES

Thai Chicken with Basil, page 23

# QUICK FROM SCRATCH
# HERBS & SPICES

Food & Wine
BOOKS

American Express Publishing Corporation
New York

**Editor in Chief:** Judith Hill

**Art Director:** Nina Scerbo
**Managing Editor:** Terri Mauro
**Editorial Assistant:** Evette Manners
**Copy Editor:** Barbara A. Mateer
**Wine Editor:** Mary Ewing-Mulligan
**Portrait Photographer:** Chris Dinerman

**Associate Editor:** Susan Lantzius Rich
**Assistant Editor:** Laura Byrne Russell
**Photographer:** Melanie Acevedo
**Food Stylist:** Rori Spinelli
**Prop Stylist:** Robyn Glaser
**Production Manager:** Stuart Handelman

**Senior Vice President/Chief Marketing Officer:** Mark V. Stanich
**Vice President, Books and Products:** Marshall A. Corey
**Marketing Manager:** Bruce Spanier
**Senior Fulfillment Manager:** Phil Black
**Business Manager:** Doreen Camardi
**Marketing Coordinator:** Richard Nogueira

**Cover Design:** Perri DeFino and Elizabeth Rendfleisch
**Recipe Pictured on Front Cover:** Thai Chicken with Basil, page 23

AMERICAN EXPRESS PUBLISHING CORPORATION
© 1998, 2002, 2004 American Express Publishing Corporation
All rights reserved. No part of this book may be reproduced or transmitted in any form or
by any means, electronic or mechanical, including photocopying, recording, or by any information storage
and retrieval system, without permission in writing from the publisher.

LIBRARY OF CONGRESS CATALOGING-IN-PUBLICATION DATA AVAILABLE

ISBN 0-916103-91-9

Published by American Express Publishing Corporation
1120 Avenue of the Americas, New York, NY 10036

Printed in China.

# CONTENTS

**RECIPES PICTURED ABOVE:** *(left to right)* pages 61, 47, 169

Checking out the flavors of fresh herbs in the FOOD & WINE Books test kitchen.

*Susan Lantzius Rich* trained at La Varenne École de Cuisine in Paris, worked as a chef in Portugal for a year, and then headed to New York City. There she made her mark first as head decorator at the well-known Sant Ambroeus pastry shop and next as a pastry chef, working at such top restaurants as San Domenico and Maxim's. In 1993, she turned her talents to recipe development and editorial work for FOOD & WINE Books.

*Judith Hill* is the editor in chief of FOOD & WINE Books, a division of American Express Publishing. Previously she was editor in chief of COOK'S Magazine, director of publications for La Varenne École de Cuisine in Paris, from which she earned a Grand Diplôme, and an English instructor for the University of Maryland International Division in Germany. Her book credits include editing cookbooks for Fredy Girardet, Jane Grigson, Michel Guérard, and Anne Willan.

*Laura Byrne Russell* earned a bachelor's degree in finance and worked in stock and bond sales for a few years before deciding that food is more fun. She went back to school, this time to The Culinary School at Kendall College in Illinois. After gaining experience in professional kitchens in Chicago and New York City, she came to FOOD & WINE Books, where she works as both an editor and a recipe developer.

# THE TASTE OF HERBS AND SPICES

We've all been known to use herbs and spices without a clue as to their real flavor or effect. We fling a bay leaf into the stew or a few juniper berries into the sauerkraut as a matter of habit, not realizing that the clean, acerbic, somewhat bitter bay contributes to the depth and complexity of the stew's flavor or that the sweet, resinous juniper helps both to mellow the sourness of kraut and to add a subtle intricacy to the taste.

To make the most of herbs and spices, you must get to know them fairly intimately. And giving you an opportunity to do just that is the main point of this book. Susan Rich, Laura Russell, and I have concentrated on dishes that are as quick and easy as all the other recipes in the *Quick from Scratch* series and in addition emphasize the nature of a spotlighted herb or spice.

We hope you'll find that using this volume not only helps you to make good food fast but also to learn exactly what individual herbs or spices taste like. Analyzing the flavors of each herb and spice in the course of developing the book gave us a lot of surprises. Marjoram and oregano are close relatives (oregano's the wild version) and taste essentially the same, but marjoram is best fresh, losing much of its flavor when dried, while oregano is actually better dried. Celery seeds are exceptionally bitter, and we learned to add them with discretion; whereas juniper berries are so sweet that I can nibble them like candy . . . well, almost. And dill seeds don't taste like dill at all, more like caraway.

In order to give you the full effect of fresh leafy herbs, we've often used rather a large quantity. So these dishes can also give you ideas for what to do with a windfall of fresh basil or how to use up some of that ever spreading mint in your garden.

Try tasting a bit of the herb or a pinch of the spice before you cook with it, and let us know about your own discoveries.

Judith Hill
Editor in Chief
FOOD & WINE Books

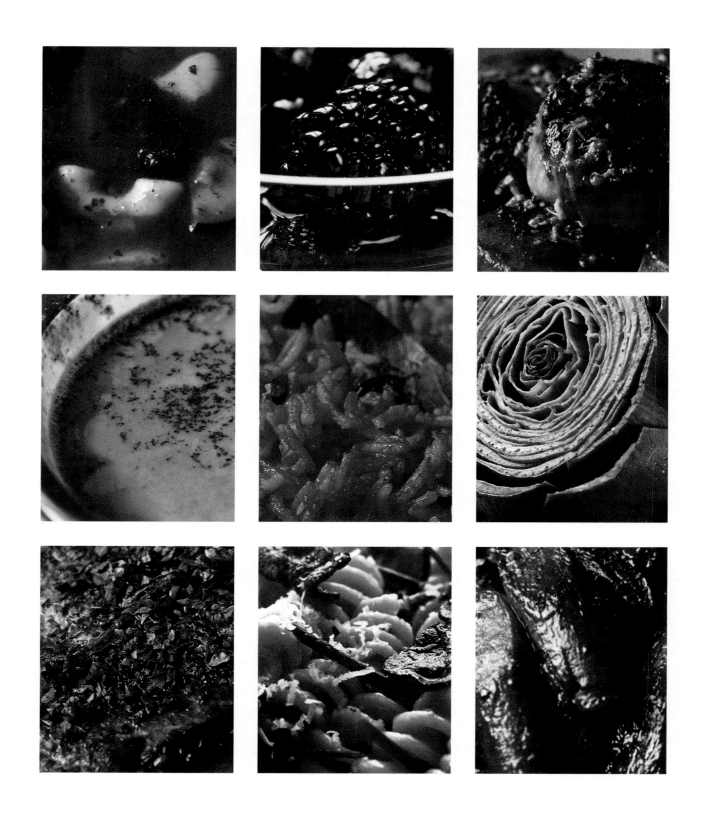

# Before You Begin

In this opening section, we've gathered thoughts and tips that apply to all, or at least a substantial number, of the recipes in this book. These are the facts and opinions that we'd like you to know before you use the recipes and hope you'll keep in mind while you use them. In addition to test-kitchen tips, you'll find information about wines and a list of recipes arranged by course rather than organized alphabetically by the herb or spice, as is the book itself.

RECIPES PICTURED OPPOSITE: (top) pages 25, 55, 83; (center) pages 95, 165, 31; (bottom) pages 69, 33, 51

# Essential Ingredient Information

### Broth, Chicken
We tested the recipes in this book using canned low-sodium chicken broth. You can almost always substitute regular for low-sodium broth; just cut back on the salt in the recipe. And if you keep homemade stock in your freezer, by all means feel free to use it. We aren't suggesting that it won't work as well, only that we know the dishes taste delicious even when made with canned broth.

### Butter
Most of our recipes don't specify whether to use salted or unsalted butter. We generally use unsalted, but in savory dishes, it really won't make a big difference which type you use.

### Garlic
The size of garlic cloves varies tremendously. When we call for one minced or chopped clove, we expect you to get about three-quarters of a teaspoon.

### Oil
*Cooking oil* in these recipes refers to readily available, reasonably priced nut, seed, or vegetable oil with a high smoking point, such as peanut, sunflower, canola, safflower, or corn oil. These can be heated to about 400° before they begin to smoke, break down, and develop an unpleasant flavor.

### Tomatoes, Canned
In some recipes, we call for "crushed tomatoes in thick puree." Depending on the brand, this mix of crushed tomatoes and tomato puree may be labeled crushed tomatoes with puree, with added puree, in tomato puree, thick style, or in thick puree. You can use any of these.

### Wine, Dry White
Leftover wine is ideal for cooking. It seems a shame to open a fresh bottle for just a few spoonfuls. Another solution is to keep dry vermouth on hand. You can use whatever quantity is needed; the rest will keep indefinitely.

### Zest
Citrus zest—the colored part of the peel, without any white pith—adds tremendous flavor to many a dish. Remove the zest from the fruit using either a grater or a zester. A zester is a small, inexpensive, and extremely handy tool. It has little holes that remove just the zest in fine ribbons. A zester is quick, easy to clean, and never scrapes your knuckles.

# PAIRING WINE WITH HERBS AND SPICES

*by Mary Ewing-Mulligan*

We all want to serve the right wine with dinner—a wine that complements the food so perfectly that the whole meal sings or, more practically, a wine that just tastes really good with the dishes we've made. When you're having a quick dinner, however, your choice of wine will probably be dictated by such mundane considerations as price and which wines are available at your neighborhood wine shop as much as by the harmony of the food-and-wine pairing. For that reason, all of the recommendations in this book are for wines that are affordable and easy to find.

If you prefer to make your own choices, these basic principles can help you make wise wine picks:

■ **Herbs and spices** contribute particular flavors to a dish, but the other ingredients come into play in determining its ultimate flavor. Characteristics such as the intensity of flavor, the richness or lightness, and the texture of the food contribute to the experience, or taste, of the dish.

■ **Wines** have specific flavors as well, and the complete taste of each wine is affected by its weight (how light-bodied or full-bodied it is), texture (crisp, soft, velvety, or rough, for example), and intensity. A wine can enhance a dish by matching its intensity, richness, texture, and flavors—or, in many cases, by contrasting some of these aspects.

■ **Herbs** generally have somewhat delicate flavors, and many recipes that feature herbs are thus rather subtle. White wines, which tend to be lighter than reds, go best with such dishes. Rosés can be fairly delicate and thus can also go well with herbal dishes.

■ **Spices** are often powerful, and a spicy dish therefore frequently needs a bold wine. Generally speaking, red wines are more assertive than whites or rosés.

■ **White wines** that have been fermented or aged in oak, as are most California chardonnays, have more intense flavor and are richer than most unoaked whites. These wines can be delicious with richer herb-flavored dishes or with lighter spicy dishes.

*Mary Ewing-Mulligan is director of the International Wine Center and co-author of* Wine for Dummies.

# RECIPES ARRANGED BY COURSE

## Main Dishes

### Fish and Shellfish

- Grilled Swordfish Kabobs, *page 29*
- Steamed Salmon with Ginger and Chives, *page 35*
- Shrimp in Coconut Milk, *page 39*
- Catfish and Potatoes with Salsa Verde, *page 67*
- Grilled Trout with Savory Marinade, *page 79*
- Scallops with Tarragon Butter Sauce, *page 83*
- Roasted Cod and Potatoes with Thyme, *page 89*
- Mussels Steamed in Tomato Broth with Goat Cheese, *page 107*
- Shrimp Boil, *page 117*
- Sautéed Catfish with Mustard Sauce, *page 147*
- Monkfish Couscous, *page 167*

### Poultry

- Thai Chicken with Basil, *page 23*
- Thai Grilled Chicken with Cilantro Dipping Sauce, *page 41*
- Chicken Potpie, *page 53*
- Cardamom Chicken with Rice Pilaf, *page 105*
- Couscous-Stuffed Cornish Hens, *page 113*
- Braised Chicken Thighs with Sauerkraut, *page 143*
- Chicken Breasts with Charmoula, *page 153*
- Chicken and Sausage Jambalaya, *page 163*
- Chinese Poached Chicken Breasts with Star Anise, *page 171*

### Meat

- Steak Pizzaiola, *page 61*
- Veal Chops with Gremolada, *page 69*
- Lamb Chops with Rosemary and Grapes, *page 73*
- Stir-Fried Pork with Carrots and Bok Choy, *page 109*
- Beef Curry, *page 119*
- Pork Tenderloin with Port and Prunes, *page 121*
- Cumin Chili, *page 125*
- Lamb Meatballs with Cumin, Mint, and Tomato Sauce, *page 127*
- Baked Sausages, Fennel, and Potatoes with Fontina, *page 135*
- Smoked Pork Chops Stuffed with Gruyère and Mustard, *page 145*

### Vegetables

- Spinach, Feta, and Tarragon Frittata, *page 85*
- Vegetable Couscous, *page 101*
- Cauliflower, Potato, and Pea Curry, *page 175*

## Side Dishes

## Desserts

## Beverages

# *Faster, Better, Easier*
## TEST-KITCHEN TIPS

### What's an herb, what's a spice?

Both herbs and spices come from plants—sometimes from the same plant. It's which *part* of that plant that makes the difference. Herbs, for example basil, cilantro, and tarragon, are the leaves of plants. Spices can be seeds (such as fennel), seed pods (cardamom), flowers (saffron), berries (juniper), buds (cloves), rhizomes (ginger), even bark (cinnamon)—just about any part of a plant *except* the leaves.

### Fresh vs. dried

Many people assume fresh herbs must be better than dried, but that's not always the case. Often, dried are just as good, and sometimes they're even better. We give you a choice in many of our recipes, with our preference listed first.

### The tough herb

Fresh rosemary leaves can be chewy—an unpleasant mouthful. Chop them fine or use whole sprigs to infuse long-simmered dishes with flavor and then remove the sprigs before serving.

### Grow your own

Herbs growing close at hand in a kitchen window are a delight, but many an indoor herb has expired from lack of light or moisture. Those most likely to survive have tough stems and small leathery leaves. Try growing rosemary and thyme rather than basil and tarragon.

### Cook most fresh herbs briefly

Adding fresh herbs too early, especially delicate-leaved herbs such as cilantro, basil, and tarragon, can rob them of flavor and color, so add them toward the end of cooking. Rosemary is an exception; it needs some heat to soften the tough leaves. Parsley too can be put in early to meld with the other ingredients, but you'll frequently want to boost its flavor and appearance by adding more just before serving.

### Dried herbs taste stronger

When substituting dried herbs for fresh, keep in mind that the former are much stronger than the latter; don't use an equal amount. As a general rule, one teaspoon of dried herbs is roughly equivalent in flavor to one tablespoon of chopped fresh herbs, and vice versa. You'll need to add dried herbs earlier in the cooking process, however, to give them time to release their flavor.

## Dried herbs: ground vs. leaf

Many dried herbs are available in both whole-leaf and ground forms. With the exception of sage, we use whole-leaf dried herbs since they retain their flavor better.

## Crumble dried herbs

To get maximum flavor from whole-leaf dried herbs such as oregano and thyme, crumble them into the dish while it's cooking. The herbs will need about fifteen minutes to rehydrate and begin to release their flavor.

## Grind your own

Whole spices keep their flavor longer than ground ones, so for top-notch flavor, buy spices whole and grind them yourself as needed. A grater works best for nutmeg. For other spices, you can do it the old-fashioned way, with a mortar and pestle, or take the easy way and put them in an electric coffee grinder (we recommend that you keep one exclusively for spices). Clean the grinder in between different spices by grinding some granulated sugar or raw rice in it and then wiping it out.

## Buying dried herbs and spices

There's no sense in stocking up on dried herbs and spices; they'll lose their flavor long before you use them up. For optimum freshness, buy the smallest quantity possible.

## Are they fresh?

There's an easy way to determine the freshness of dried herbs and spices: Smell them. If the aroma is faint or nonexistent, the flavor will be, too. It's not a crime to throw out old herbs and spices. Most are not what they should be after a year on your shelf.

## Spoon, don't sprinkle

Use a measuring spoon or your hand to add dried herbs and spices to a simmering pot. Though it may be tempting to just sprinkle some in straight from the jar, you may be sacrificing your remaining supply—the rising steam can cause the rest of the contents of the jar to lose flavor and to clump.

## Using whole spices

Since whole spices such as cinnamon sticks or star anise release flavor more slowly than ground ones, they are best used in dishes that require long-simmering.

## Toasting ground spices

To enhance the flavor of ground spices, you can toast them in a dry frying pan. They burn quickly, so keep a sharp eye on them and stir them constantly; the toasting should take less than a minute. If the spices do burn, they'll make any dish bitter. Discard them and begin again.

# Storing Herbs and Spices

## Dried Herbs and Spices

■ **Dried herbs and spices** keep best stored in airtight containers in a cool, dark place. Light causes them to fade and heat reduces their flavor, so the worst possible place to keep them is above the stove.

■ **Red spices**, such as chili powder, paprika, and cayenne, can also be kept in a cool, dark place, but if you want to be especially careful to retain freshness, put them in the refrigerator.

## Fresh Herbs

■ **Most fresh herbs** will last anywhere from several days to a week or two in the refrigerator. Store them either in a perforated plastic bag or wrapped loosely in paper towels (to absorb the moisture) and tucked inside a regular plastic bag.

■ **Basil** turns brown quickly when it's cooped up in plastic, so store it with the stems immersed in water, like a bouquet of flowers. Keep the basil either on the counter or in the refrigerator.

■ **Cilantro** will also benefit from being stored with its stems in water. Put the bunch in the refrigerator and cap it with a plastic bag left loose around the bottom to keep the leaves in a humid atmosphere but allow for air circulation.

**When to wash:** Most herbs shouldn't be washed until you're ready to use them. Storing herbs with moisture clinging to the leaves definitely hastens their demise. Hardy herbs like parsley can be washed before storing, but be sure to dry them well.

**Preserving:** What to do with an abundance of fresh herbs? You can put the sprigs or leaves in a single layer on a rack or a piece of wire mesh and leave them in a warm room until **dry**, about five days. Store the dried herbs in an airtight container. Or, you can **freeze** the herbs: Fill ice-cube trays halfway with chopped fresh herbs and then with water. Freeze, remove the cubes from the tray, and store in freezer bags for up to six months. Fresh chives can even be frozen whole; just cut off as much as you need without defrosting.

# HERB AND SPICE SUBSTITUTIONS

| | SUBSTITUTE | COMMENTS |
|---|---|---|
| BASIL | mint | Both are members of the mint family. |
| CHIVES | scallion tops | Both have a mild onion flavor. |
| LEMONGRASS | lemon zest | Use one $1/2$-by-3-inch piece of lemon zest for each stalk of lemongrass. |
| MARJORAM | oregano | The two herbs can be used almost interchangeably. Oregano is stronger, so use less. |
| MINT | basil | Both are members of the mint family. |
| OREGANO | marjoram | These herbs can be used almost interchangeably. Marjoram is milder, so use more. |
| TARRAGON | chervil | Both are delicate with a mild anise flavor. Chervil is milder, so use more. |

| | SUBSTITUTE | COMMENTS |
|---|---|---|
| ALLSPICE | cloves | Cloves are stronger; cut the quantity to one quarter. |
| CELERY SEEDS | celery salt | In a pinch, use celery salt; just omit the salt in the recipe. |
| CARAWAY SEEDS | dill seeds | Though somewhat different in taste, they are of equal strength and so can be substituted in the same quantity. |
| CINNAMON | allspice | Allspice, in a smaller quantity, can be used in cakes, cookies, and pies, and with apples, squash, and pumpkin. |
| CLOVES | allspice | Allspice is milder; use three-quarters more. |
| DILL SEEDS | caraway seeds | Though somewhat different in taste, they are of equal strength and so can be substituted in the same quantity. |
| FENNEL SEEDS | aniseeds | In addition, Pernod can substitute for fennel or aniseeds. Sweetened anise liqueurs such as anisette work in puddings, custards, and cookies. |
| GINGER | gingerroot | Substitute grated fresh gingerroot for a slightly hotter ginger flavor. You'll need three-quarters more. |
| JUNIPER BERRIES | gin | Use a tablespoon of gin for every two or three juniper berries. |
| MUSTARD POWDER | prepared mustard | Use about one tablespoon prepared mustard for each teaspoon of mustard powder. |
| RED PEPPER | chili oil, Tabasco sauce | Start with a little and taste. |
| STAR ANISE | fennel or aniseeds | The seeds will lack the complexity of flavor and may need to be strained out. |

HERB

SPICE

# Herbs

## Tarragon

## Thyme

## BASIL

*It may be best known as the herb that puts the green in pesto, but with its enchanting fragrance and hints of mint, licorice, and clove, basil can bring excitement to all manner of dishes. A member of the mint family, basil comes in many varieties. Sweet is the most common; others include lemon, cinnamon, the purple-hued opal, and holy basil, which is commonly used in Thai cooking. Whatever kind you choose, it should be fresh; in the process of drying, the flavor seems to evaporate from the leaves along with the moisture. Because heat also destroys the flavor, add basil generously at the end of cooking.* 🌿 **USES** *Basil is at its peak in the summer and is well paired with summer vegetables like eggplant, peppers, and zucchini. It's never better, though, than with tomatoes. Top sliced tomatoes with basil and a splash of vinegar for a simple salad, or use chopped rather than sliced tomatoes in the same combination for a tasty no-cook pasta sauce. Fold chopped basil into unsweetened whipped cream, and swirl the cream into tomato soup. Try also: stuffing chicken breasts with basil and goat cheese; mixing chopped basil with butter to top a grilled steak or chop; using basil in place of lettuce on sandwiches.*

# THAI CHICKEN WITH BASIL

An abundance of whole basil leaves joins chicken and fiery red chiles for a quick, delicious, and decidedly spicy stir-fry. Holy basil is the most authentic choice, but any variety will do.

**WINE RECOMMENDATION**
Look for a rich but dry white wine, such as a pinot gris from the Alsace region in France.

**SERVES 4**

1⅓  pounds boneless, skinless chicken breasts (about 4), cut into 1-by-2-inch pieces

2  tablespoons Asian fish sauce (nam pla or nuoc mam)*

1½  tablespoons soy sauce

1  tablespoon water

1½  teaspoons sugar

2  tablespoons cooking oil

1  large onion, cut into thin slices

3  fresh red chiles, seeds and ribs removed, cut into thin slices, or ¼ teaspoon dried red-pepper flakes

3  cloves garlic, minced

1½  cups lightly packed basil leaves

*Available at Asian markets and many supermarkets

1. In a medium bowl, combine the chicken with the fish sauce, soy sauce, water, and sugar. In a large nonstick frying pan or a wok, heat the oil over moderately high heat. Add the onion and cook, stirring, for 2 minutes. Stir in the chiles and garlic; cook, stirring, 30 seconds longer.

2. Remove the chicken from the marinade with a slotted spoon and add it to the hot pan. Cook until almost done, stirring, about 3 minutes. Add the marinade and cook 30 seconds longer. Remove from the heat and stir in 1 cup of the basil. Serve topped with the remaining ½ cup basil.

# SOUPE AU PISTOU

Much like pesto, its Italian cousin, French *pistou* is a mixture of basil, garlic, and olive oil. Here we stir some into a hearty Provençal soup made with vegetables, potatoes, beans, and pasta and spoon the rest on top.

**WINE RECOMMENDATION**
A good German riesling will cut through the richness of the soup and refresh your palate with its lively flavor. Try a kabinett or spätlese wine, preferably halbtrocken (on the dry side).

**SERVES 4**

6 tablespoons olive oil

1 large onion, chopped

2 carrots, chopped

1 zucchini (about ½ pound), quartered lengthwise, cut crosswise into thin slices

¼ pound green beans, cut into 1-inch lengths

2 teaspoons salt

¼ teaspoon fresh-ground black pepper

1 pound boiling potatoes, peeled and cut into ½-inch dice

1½ cups drained canned diced tomatoes (one 15-ounce can)

1 quart canned low-sodium chicken broth or homemade stock

3 cups water

1 cup drained and rinsed canned white beans, preferably cannellini

½ cup elbow macaroni or other small pasta

3 small cloves garlic, peeled

1 cup loosely packed basil leaves

1. In a large pot, heat 2 tablespoons of the oil over moderately low heat. Add the onion and carrots and cook, stirring occasionally, until the onions are translucent, about 5 minutes. Add the zucchini, green beans, ¾ teaspoon of the salt, and the pepper and cook, stirring occasionally, until the vegetables start to soften, about 5 minutes longer.

2. Add the potatoes, tomatoes, broth, and water and bring to a boil. Reduce the heat and simmer 15 minutes. Add the beans, pasta, and 1 teaspoon of the salt. Continue simmering until the vegetables are tender and the pasta is cooked through, about 10 minutes longer. Remove from the heat.

3. Meanwhile, in a blender or food processor, puree the garlic, basil, and the remaining 4 tablespoons oil and ¼ teaspoon salt. Stir ¼ cup of this *pistou* into the soup. Serve the soup topped with the remaining *pistou*.

# LINGUINE WITH RATATOUILLE SAUCE

The vegetables that make up traditional Provençal ratatouille—eggplant, zucchini, tomatoes, and bell peppers—all go particularly well with basil. We've turned them into a pasta sauce that can also be served on polenta or on a hero with sausages.

**WINE RECOMMENDATION**
The combined acidity of tomatoes and vinegar calls for a crisp, high-acid wine—one with enough earthiness to complement the vegetables. An unoaked chardonnay from northeastern Italy fills the bill.

**SERVES 4**

- 3 tablespoons olive oil
- 1 onion, cut into thin slices
- 1 green or red bell pepper, cut into 1/2-inch dice
- 1 small eggplant (about 1/2 pound), cut into 1/2-inch dice
- 1 zucchini (about 1/2 pound), cut into 1/2-inch dice
- 3 cloves garlic, chopped
- 1 1/4 teaspoons salt
- 1/2 teaspoon fresh-ground black pepper
- 1 2/3 cups canned crushed tomatoes in thick puree (one 15-ounce can)
- 2 teaspoons wine vinegar
- 3/4 pound linguine
- 1/2 cup plus 2 tablespoons thin-sliced basil leaves

1. In a large frying pan, heat the oil over moderate heat. Add the onion and bell pepper and cook, stirring occasionally, until the onion is translucent, about 5 minutes. Add the eggplant, zucchini, garlic, salt, and black pepper. Reduce the heat to moderately low and cook, covered, for 15 minutes, stirring occasionally.

2. Add the tomatoes and simmer, covered, stirring occasionally, until the vegetables are tender, about 10 minutes. Stir in the vinegar.

3. In a large pot of boiling, salted water, cook the linguine until just done, about 12 minutes. Reserve about 1/2 cup of the pasta-cooking water. Drain the pasta and toss with the vegetables, the 1/2 cup basil, and, if the pasta seems too dry, some of the reserved pasta-cooking water. Serve topped with the 2 tablespoons basil.

## BAY LEAVES

*Age improves bay leaves—up to a point. Fresh leaves, though certainly usable, can be bitter. Let them dehydrate a bit and they'll be the better for it. Fully dried bay actually has more flavor than fresh. Just don't let it sit on your shelf so long that no aroma remains. The long, narrow leaves of California bay are stronger and more bitter than the shorter, rounder leaves of the Mediterranean variety. We prefer the mellow Mediterranean. If you use California bay, reduce the quantity called for in our recipes by half. Though bay leaves impart wonderful flavor, they're not generally eaten themselves.* **USES** *Bay, also called sweet laurel and sweet bay, originated in the Mediterranean and is an essential herb in European cuisines. The leaf keeps dispensing flavor throughout long simmering. It's a good addition to stocks, soups, stews, and sauces, either alone or with thyme and parsley in a bouquet garni. Try also: using bay leaves in macerated vegetables, such as vegetables à la grecque, or in marinades for grilling; adding bay leaves to pilafs and rice dishes; flavoring dessert custards with bay leaves.*

# GRILLED SWORDFISH KABOBS

Bay leaves interspersed with chunks of swordfish in these bread-crumb-coated kabobs add another taste dimension to the fish as it cooks. Tuna or salmon would benefit from the same treatment. Be sure to keep the heat of the grill at low to moderately low so the crumbs don't burn.

**WINE RECOMMENDATION**
A medium-bodied pinot noir from Oregon or California or a Bourgogne Rouge from France will be ideal with swordfish.

**SERVES 4**

1½ pounds swordfish steaks, about 1 inch thick, cut into 1-inch cubes

About 30 bay leaves

4½ tablespoons olive oil

¼ cup dry bread crumbs

2 tablespoons chopped flat-leaf parsley

¾ teaspoon salt

½ teaspoon fresh-ground black pepper

1. Light the grill or heat the broiler. Thread the fish cubes alternately with the bay leaves onto four large skewers. Put the kabobs on a plate and brush them all over with 3 tablespoons of the oil.

2. On a large plate, combine the bread crumbs, parsley, salt, and pepper. Holding the kabobs over the plate, pat the crumbs onto the exposed sides of the fish. Drizzle with the oil left on the first plate and sprinkle with any crumbs that didn't stick.

3. Grill the kabobs over low to moderately low heat or broil them, brushing with the remaining 1½ tablespoons oil, until the bread crumbs are golden and the fish is just done, 8 to 10 minutes.

# ARTICHOKES WITH SCALLION VINAIGRETTE

A generous portion of bay leaves in the steaming liquid here permeates the artichoke leaves and hearts with flavor and provides an enticing aroma as you serve the dish. The scallion vinaigrette balances the sweetness of the artichokes.

**SERVES 4**

|       |                                      |
|-------|--------------------------------------|
| 1     | quart water                          |
| 1     | cup plus 2 tablespoons olive oil     |
| 5½    | tablespoons wine vinegar             |
| 1     | small onion, cut into thin slices    |
| 12    | peppercorns                          |
| 5     | bay leaves                           |
| 1½    | teaspoons salt                       |
| 4     | large artichokes                     |
| 2     | teaspoons Dijon mustard              |
| 4     | scallions including green tops, chopped |
| 6     | tablespoons chopped fresh parsley    |
| 1¼    | teaspoons lemon juice                |
| ½     | teaspoon fresh-ground black pepper    |

1. In a large wide stainless-steel pot, combine the water, the 2 tablespoons oil, 1½ tablespoons of the vinegar, the onion, peppercorns, bay leaves, and ¼ teaspoon of the salt. Bring to a boil.

2. Cut the stems off the artichokes and cut off the top third of the leaves. If you like, using scissors, cut off the tips from the remaining leaves to remove the thorns. Put the artichokes in the pot, stem ends down. Cover and bring back to a boil. Reduce the heat and simmer until the bases of the artichokes are tender when pierced with a small knife, 30 to 40 minutes. Remove the artichokes.

3. In a small glass or stainless-steel bowl, whisk together the mustard, the remaining 4 tablespoons vinegar, the scallions, parsley, lemon juice, the remaining 1¼ teaspoons salt, and the ground pepper. Add the remaining 1 cup oil slowly, whisking. Serve each artichoke with a small bowl of vinaigrette alongside for dipping.

 **CHIVES** *Proud to proclaim its heritage as an upstanding member of the onion family, the herb called chives boasts a clear, though mild, onion flavor. It bears a subtle scent of garlic, too. Chinese chives, also known as garlic chives, have a garlicky taste as well as scent. Fresh chives look like long, hollow blades of grass and sometimes come with a lavender blossom attached. This flower is perfectly edible and tastes even more oniony than the chive stems themselves. Chives hold their flavor best when cooked very little or not at all. And they must be fresh; drying obliterates their flavor.*

**USES** *Chives, along with parsley, chervil, and tarragon, are part of the fines herbes quartet—a classic addition to egg, fish, and chicken dishes. Sprinkle chives over potato and cheddar-cheese soup for a hearty winter meal, or throw a handful into a stir-fry of beef and cherry tomatoes. Toss the flowers into a salad or fry them to make a tasty garnish. Try also: topping sautéed chicken or trout and mustard cream sauce with a shower of chives; adding plenty of chives to corn chowder; including chives in a frittata with bacon and Parmesan; using them to brighten a cauliflower or potato gratin.*

# FUSILLI WITH BACON AND CHIVES

Fry a few slices of bacon, boil some fusilli, and you have the makings of a sumptuous pasta dish that's ready to go in next to no time. The chives keep all their spark because they aren't cooked at all; they're tossed in with the butter and Parmesan that so temptingly coat the pasta. If you really love the smoky taste of bacon, replace some of the butter with fat rendered during cooking.

**WINE RECOMMENDATION**
To add a lively note to this delicious pasta, try a white wine that has a good, crisp acidity. A sauvignon blanc from New Zealand would be perfect.

**SERVES 4**

⅓ pound bacon, slices cut crosswise into
  1-inch pieces

¾ pound fusilli

½ cup grated Parmesan, plus more for serving

3 tablespoons butter, cut into pieces

½ cup 1-inch pieces fresh chives

¼ teaspoon salt

¼ teaspoon fresh-ground black pepper

1. In a large frying pan, cook the pieces of bacon until they are golden brown and crisp. Using a slotted spoon, remove the bacon from the pan and drain it on paper towels.

2. In a large pot of boiling, salted water, cook the fusilli until done, about 13 minutes. Reserve ½ cup of the cooking water and drain the pasta.

3. Toss the pasta with the Parmesan until thoroughly combined. Stir in ¼ cup of the reserved pasta-cooking water, the bacon, butter, chives, salt, and pepper. Stir in more of the reserved pasta-cooking water if needed to make the dish moist. Serve topped with additional Parmesan.

# STEAMED SALMON WITH GINGER AND CHIVES

Chives do double duty in this simple salmon dish: They're in the marinade and also sprinkled atop the finished fish as a final flash of flavor. Cook the salmon in a steamer basket placed in a pot, as we do here; in a wok fitted with a bamboo steamer basket, as is traditional in China; or on a plate set atop a metal ring (such as a tuna can with both ends removed) in a large wide pot containing about one inch of water.

**WINE RECOMMENDATION**
The rich salmon and other bold ingredients can stand up to a lusty, fruity California chardonnay, or, if you prefer to serve a red wine, a full-bodied merlot.

**SERVES 4**

- 3   tablespoons sake or dry white wine
- 2   tablespoons soy sauce
- 1   teaspoon Asian sesame oil
- 3   cloves garlic, minced
- 1   1½-inch piece fresh ginger, peeled and cut into matchstick strips
- 2   tablespoons chopped fresh chives
- ¾   teaspoon sugar
- ¼   teaspoon dried red-pepper flakes
- ¼   teaspoon fresh-ground black pepper
- 4   salmon steaks, about 1 inch thick (about 2 pounds in all)

1. In a small glass or stainless-steel bowl, combine the sake, soy sauce, sesame oil, garlic, ginger, 1 tablespoon of the chives, the sugar, red-pepper flakes, and black pepper. Put the salmon steaks, in one layer, in a shallow Pyrex dish and pour the soy mixture over it.

2. In a large pot, bring about 1 inch of water to a boil over high heat. Put the dish with the fish and sauce in a large steamer basket. Put the basket over the boiling water and cover. Reduce the heat to moderately high and cook until the salmon is just barely done (the fish should still be translucent in the center), about 10 minutes. Serve the salmon steaks with the cooking juices poured over them and the remaining 1 tablespoon chives sprinkled on top.

## FISH ALTERNATIVES

You can use firm white fish fillets such as **red snapper, grouper,** or **sea bass.** Cook them until the center is opaque.

**CILANTRO** *Confused about the relationship between cilantro and coriander? They both refer to the same plant, which is named* coriander. *The leaves, stems, and root of the plant are usually called* cilantro *(though sometimes fresh coriander or Chinese parsley); the seeds are dried and ground and always referred to as* coriander *(see page 119). Most people clarify matters by calling the herb* cilantro *and the spice* coriander. *The herb should be very fresh; its flavor, though strong, begins to lessen as soon as the stems are picked. Try to buy it with the roots attached so that you are in effect picking it yourself as needed. Because of their fast-fading flavor, cilantro leaves are best added at the last minute. Most cilantro-loving cuisines stick to the leaves, but the roots are used, too, primarily in Thai and Indonesian cooking.* ❦ **USES** *Native to southern Europe, the Middle East, and the Far East, cilantro is one of the more widespread herbs. It has become de rigueur in or on top of a multitude of Mexican dishes. Try also: adding leaves to yogurt, fresh chutney, and relishes; stirring them into tomato sauce; tossing them into stir-fries or salads; floating them on soups.*

# CHICKEN, MANGO, AND RICE SALAD

Mango and avocado may seem unlikely partners, but they have one thing in common: an affinity for cilantro. Here the herb ties them together in an unusual and unusually delicious dish. The salad makes a fine light meal all by itself.

**WINE RECOMMENDATION**
With its fruit, richness, and flavor, Australian sémillon will match this dish blow for blow.

**SERVES 4**

| | |
|---|---|
| $1\frac{1}{2}$ | cups rice, preferably short grain |
| $1\frac{1}{3}$ | pounds boneless, skinless chicken breasts (about 4 ) |
| $\frac{1}{3}$ | cup plus 1 tablespoon cooking oil |
| $1\frac{1}{4}$ | teaspoons salt |
| $\frac{3}{4}$ | teaspoon fresh-ground black pepper |
| $\frac{3}{4}$ | cup chopped red onion |
| 1 | mango, peeled and cut into $\frac{1}{2}$-inch dice |
| 1 | avocado, peeled and cut into $\frac{1}{2}$-inch dice |
| $3\frac{1}{2}$ | tablespoons lime juice (from about 2 limes) |
| $\frac{3}{4}$ | cup chopped cilantro |

1. In a large pot of boiling, salted water, cook the rice until just done, 10 to 15 minutes. Drain. Rinse with cold water. Drain thoroughly.

2. Coat the chicken with the 1 tablespoon oil. Season with $\frac{1}{4}$ teaspoon each of the salt and pepper. Heat a grill pan over moderate heat. Cook the breasts until just done, 4 to 5 minutes per side. Alternatively, heat the tablespoon of oil in a large frying pan and season and cook the chicken as directed above. When the chicken is cool enough to handle, cut it into $\frac{1}{2}$-inch dice.

3. Toss the rice with the chicken, onion, mango, avocado, the $\frac{1}{3}$ cup oil, the remaining 1 teaspoon salt and $\frac{1}{2}$ teaspoon pepper, the lime juice, and cilantro.

# SHRIMP IN COCONUT MILK

Coconut and cilantro are a popular duo. The herb is a favorite in India and shows up in coconut chutneys and in many of southern India's coconut curries, such as this one. Serve the shrimp with steamed rice, preferably basmati.

**WINE RECOMMENDATION**
Sparkling wines go well with a wide variety of dishes. For an unexpected treat with this exotic curry, serve a good-quality bubbly from California.

**SERVES 4**

¼ cup cooking oil

2 onions, chopped fine

4 cloves garlic, minced

2 tablespoons minced fresh ginger

2 tablespoons ground coriander

¼ teaspoon ground cumin

¼ teaspoon cinnamon

⅛ teaspoon cayenne

⅛ teaspoon turmeric

1 cup drained whole canned tomatoes, cut into ½-inch pieces (from a 15-ounce can)

2½ cups canned unsweetened coconut milk (from two 15-ounce cans)

½ cup water

1¼ teaspoons salt

1½ pounds large shrimp, shelled

¾ cup chopped cilantro

Lime wedges, for serving

1. In a large frying pan, heat the oil over moderately high heat. Add the onions and cook, stirring frequently, until golden, about 5 minutes. Add the garlic and ginger and cook, stirring, for 2 minutes.

2. Add the coriander, cumin, cinnamon, cayenne, and turmeric and cook, stirring, for 30 seconds. Add the tomatoes and cook, stirring, for 1 minute. Add the coconut milk, water, and salt and bring to a simmer. Reduce the heat and cook at a low boil, stirring frequently, until thickened, 5 to 10 minutes.

3. Add the shrimp to the pan. Reduce the heat to low and bring to a simmer. Cook, stirring occasionally, until the shrimp are just done, 3 to 5 minutes. Remove from the heat and stir in the cilantro. Serve with the lime wedges.

# THAI GRILLED CHICKEN WITH CILANTRO DIPPING SAUCE

Cilantro stems get in the act in this recipe; they're pureed with the leaves, jalapeños, garlic, fish sauce, and sesame oil to make a flavorful coating for grilled chicken. The dipping sauce, which also contains cilantro, is a classic Thai sweet-and-sour sauce.

**WINE RECOMMENDATION**
The rich, unctuous texture and pronounced fruity flavor of a dry gewürztraminer from France's Alsace region will provide a lovely contrast to these strong, spicy flavors.

**SERVES 4**

2   jalapeño peppers, seeds and ribs removed

4   cloves garlic, 2 smashed, 2 minced

1/2 cup lightly packed cilantro leaves and stems, plus 1 tablespoon chopped cilantro

2   tablespoons Asian fish sauce (nam pla or nuoc mam)*

1   tablespoon cooking oil

1   teaspoon Asian sesame oil

1/2 teaspoon salt

4   boneless, skinless chicken breasts (about 1 1/3 pounds in all)

6   tablespoons rice-wine vinegar

1   tablespoon sugar

1/4 teaspoon dried red-pepper flakes

1 1/2 tablespoons water

*Available at Asian markets and many supermarkets

1. Light the grill or heat the broiler. In a blender or food processor, puree the jalapeños, smashed garlic cloves, the 1/2 cup cilantro leaves and stems, the fish sauce, cooking oil, sesame oil, and 1/4 teaspoon of the salt. Put the chicken in a shallow dish and coat it with the cilantro puree.

2. Grill the chicken over moderately high heat or broil it for 5 minutes. Turn and cook until just done, about 5 minutes longer.

3. Meanwhile, in a small stainless-steel saucepan, bring the vinegar, sugar, and the remaining 1/4 teaspoon salt to a simmer, stirring. Simmer for 2 minutes. Pour the liquid into a small glass or stainless-steel bowl and let cool. Add the minced garlic, the 1 tablespoon chopped cilantro, the red-pepper flakes, and water. Serve each chicken breast with a small bowl of the dipping sauce alongside.

*Don't let dill's delicate appearance fool you; those wispy leaves pack plenty of flavor. Pickles are only the beginning. Toss in some of the feathery green herb at the end of cooking to raise many dishes, especially ones with a Scandinavian, Russian, or Greek heritage, to new heights. You may be able to get away with using dried dillweed in some cases, but it can't match the sprightliness of fresh. Though dill leaves resemble fennel tops, and are sometimes suggested as a substitute for them, the flavors are nothing alike.*  **USES** *Vegetables love dill. Green beans, carrots, cucumbers, and beets are especially harmonious matches. Put dill in potato salad (particularly one made with mustard), mix it with cucumbers and yogurt to make a Greek tzatziki sauce to serve over grilled fish or chicken, or make a quick pasta sauce with strips of smoked salmon, chopped tomatoes, and dill. Try also: sprinkling chopped dill over chicken noodle, tomato, or lentil soup; adding it to a green salad, an omelet, sautéed shrimp, or rice pilaf; mixing it with grated lemon zest to top sautéed lamb or veal chops; substituting chopped dill and yogurt for some of the mayonnaise in potato or chicken salad.*

# GRILLED SALMON WITH ORZO SALAD

More than one tradition is at work here. Dill and cucumber, mated in several cuisines, unite in a Greek-inspired salad, while salmon and dill are a typical Scandinavian pairing.

**WINE RECOMMENDATION**
A good Sancerre or Pouilly-Fumé will make the fresh, bright flavors of this pasta salad sing.

**SERVES 4**

1 cucumber, peeled, halved, seeded, and cut into ½-inch dice

4 plum tomatoes, cut into ½-inch dice

1 teaspoon salt

½ pound orzo (about 1 cup)

⅓ cup plus 1 tablespoon olive oil

2 tablespoons plus 1 teaspoon lemon juice

⅓ cup plus 1 tablespoon chopped fresh dill
Fresh-ground black pepper

1½ pounds salmon fillet, about 1 inch thick, cut into 4 pieces
Grated zest of ½ lemon

1. In a strainer set over a medium bowl, toss the cucumber, tomatoes, and ½ teaspoon of the salt and let drain for 15 minutes.

2. Meanwhile, in a large pot of boiling, salted water, cook the orzo until just done, about 12 minutes. Drain. Rinse with cold water and drain thoroughly. Toss the orzo with the ⅓ cup oil, the lemon juice, the ⅓ cup dill, ¼ teaspoon of the salt, ⅛ teaspoon pepper, and the cucumber and tomatoes.

3. Light the grill. Coat the salmon with the 1 tablespoon oil, the remaining ¼ teaspoon salt, and ¼ teaspoon pepper. Grill the salmon, skin-side up, for 4 minutes. Turn and sprinkle with the 1 tablespoon dill and the lemon zest. Cook the fish until golden brown and just barely done (the fish should still be translucent in the center), about 3 minutes longer. Serve the fish on the salad.

# CHUNKY BORSCHT

Brothy and brimming with beets, parsnips, turnip, celery root, and slices of kielbasa, this earthy beet soup gets a finishing touch of sour cream and fresh dill. Serve it in big bowls with plenty of crusty bread for an appetizing cold-weather dinner.

**WINE RECOMMENDATION**
California sauvignon blanc has enough intensity of taste to stand up to the borscht, and the subtly herbal nature of its flavor will accentuate the dill nicely.

**SERVES 4**

- 2 tablespoons cooking oil
- 1 onion, chopped
- 2 parsnips, peeled and cut into thin slices
- 1 small celery root (about $3/4$ pound), peeled and cut into $1/2$-inch chunks
- 1 turnip, peeled and cut into $1/2$-inch chunks
- $1^3/4$ teaspoons salt
- 2 cups drained diced canned beets (one 15-ounce can)
- $1^1/2$ cups drained diced canned tomatoes (one 15-ounce can)
- $3^1/2$ cups canned low-sodium beef broth or homemade stock
- 3 cups water
- $1/4$ teaspoon fresh-ground black pepper
- $1/2$ pound kielbasa, halved lengthwise and sliced crosswise
- $1/3$ cup plus 3 tablespoons chopped fresh dill
- $1/4$ cup sour cream

1. In a large saucepan, heat the oil over moderately low heat. Add the onion and cook, stirring occasionally, until translucent, about 5 minutes. Add the parsnips, celery root, turnip, and 1 teaspoon of the salt. Cover and cook until the vegetables start to soften, about 5 minutes.

2. Add the beets, tomatoes, broth, water, the remaining $3/4$ teaspoon salt, and the pepper. Bring to a boil. Add the kielbasa. Reduce the heat and simmer, uncovered, until the vegetables are tender, about 15 minutes. Stir in the $1/3$ cup dill. Serve topped with the sour cream and the remaining 3 tablespoons dill.

## VARIATION

Instead of the kielbasa, you can use the same amount of **Black Forest ham**, or any good smoked ham, cut into small chunks.

**LEMONGRASS** *The name of this herb pretty much sums it up: The aroma and flavor are like those of the zest from a particularly heady lemon, and the plant has a tall, narrow, grass-like stalk. Because most of the stalk is woody, use only the moist bottom third. Even that section is fibrous, so lemongrass is usually steeped in liquid to bring out the flavor or minced and used in marinades. It is available dried, but this form has little resemblance to fresh. The best substitute for fresh lemongrass is not dried lemongrass at all but lemon zest, perhaps with a touch of grated fresh ginger.* **USES** *Lemongrass is popular in cuisines throughout Southeast Asia, especially in Thailand and Vietnam. You'll find it in hot-and-sour soup and in marinades for chicken and pork satays. Try also: adding lemongrass to curries and stews featuring chicken, fish, or shellfish; infusing oil with lemongrass and using the oil for vinaigrettes; adding lemongrass to marinades for steak or lamb; steeping the cut-up stalks in milk and making a lemongrass custard with it; poaching fruit in sugar syrup with minced lemongrass; making lemongrass tea.*

# THAI CHICKEN AND COCONUT SOUP

We've deviated slightly from the classic version of a popular Thai soup by adding rice to make it more substantial. Serve it with lime wedges; a squirt at the table does wonders.

**WINE RECOMMENDATION**
Semidry German riesling proves its food-friendliness by complementing this complex soup.

**SERVES 4**

- 1 pound boneless, skinless chicken breasts (about 3), cut into 2½-by-¼-inch strips
- 3 tablespoons Asian fish sauce (nam pla or nuoc mam)*
- 1½ tablespoons lime juice
- 1 quart plus ¾ cup canned low-sodium chicken broth or homemade stock
- 3 stalks lemongrass, bottom third only, peeled, smashed, and cut into 2-inch pieces, or three 3-inch-by-¼-inch strips lemon zest
- 1 1-inch piece peeled fresh ginger, cut into thirds
- ½ cup long-grain rice
- 1¾ cups unsweetened coconut milk (15-ounce can)

- 2 fresh red chiles or jalapeño peppers, seeds and ribs removed, cut crosswise into thin slices
- 3 tablespoons chopped cilantro

  *Available at Asian markets and many supermarkets

1. In a medium glass dish or stainless-steel pan, combine the chicken strips with the fish sauce and lime juice. Set aside.

2. In a large saucepan, bring the broth, lemongrass, and ginger to a simmer. Add the rice; simmer until the rice is almost done, about 15 minutes.

3. Add the coconut milk and bring back to a simmer. Stir in the chicken and marinade and cook until the chicken is just done, about 2 minutes. Stir in the chiles and cilantro.

# BEEF SATAYS OVER THAI SALAD

The salad that lies beneath the succulent chunks of sirloin here jump-starts the taste buds—romaine, cucumber, carrots, mint, and cilantro with a Thai dressing of fish sauce, lemon juice, and rice vinegar. It's refreshing, light, and perfect for a warm summer evening.

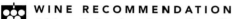

**WINE RECOMMENDATION** Although beef traditionally calls for a red, these seasonings suggest a white wine. A rich Californian, such as a full-bodied chardonnay, can play to both the beef and the salad here. If you prefer red wine, try a light, fruity Beaujolais.

**SERVES 4**

1½ pounds sirloin steak, cut into 1-inch cubes

4 stalks lemongrass, bottom third only, peeled and minced

2 cloves garlic, minced

3 tablespoons cooking oil

2½ tablespoons lemon juice

2¾ teaspoons sugar

½ teaspoon salt

¼ teaspoon fresh-ground black pepper

2 tablespoons Asian fish sauce (nam pla or nuoc mam)*

1 tablespoon water

¾ teaspoon rice-wine vinegar

Pinch dried red-pepper flakes

1 small head romaine lettuce, cut crosswise into ½-inch strips (about 1 quart)

2 carrots, grated

1 cucumber, peeled, halved, seeded, and diced

½ cup lightly packed cilantro leaves

¼ cup chopped fresh mint

*Available at Asian markets and many supermarkets

1. In a medium shallow glass or stainless-steel bowl, combine the steak, lemongrass, half the garlic, the oil, 1½ tablespoons of the lemon juice, ¾ teaspoon of the sugar, the salt, and black pepper. Set aside.

2. In a small glass or stainless-steel bowl, combine the fish sauce, the remaining 1 tablespoon lemon juice, garlic, and 2 teaspoons sugar, the water, vinegar, and red-pepper flakes.

3. In a large glass or stainless-steel bowl, combine the romaine, carrots, cucumber, cilantro, and mint.

4. Light the grill or heat the broiler. Thread the steak onto eight skewers. Grill or broil the meat, turning, until done to your taste, about 5 minutes for medium rare. Toss the dressing with the salad and serve topped with the satays.

## MARJORAM

*Sweet marjoram is quite a different herb entirely from wild marjoram, otherwise known as oregano. The two are similar enough so that they can sometimes be substituted for each other, but don't consider them as one and the same. You can distinguish marjoram by its paler flavor, aroma, and color. And whereas oregano is usually dried, marjoram is okay dried but best fresh. Marjoram's flavor has also been compared to that of thyme, and it can replace that herb as well. Though it's milder than oregano, fresh marjoram is not subtle; you'll want to use it sparingly. To avoid loss of flavor, add fresh marjoram to dishes toward the end of cooking. Dried, on the other hand, should go in early. ❦ **USES** Sautéed mushrooms taste delicious with marjoram. So does lamb, whether as grilled brochettes or in a Greek meat sauce. Try also: tossing chopped marjoram with pasta, olive oil, cooked broccoli, and sausage; adding it to chicken braised with carrots; stirring a little into fettuccine Alfredo; simmering it in a pot of beans; sautéing veal scaloppine and then deglazing the pan with a little cream and a touch of marjoram to make a quick sauce.*

# SAUTÉED CARROTS
# WITH LEMON AND MARJORAM

Lemon juice and garlic balance sweet sautéed carrots flavored with fresh marjoram. A simple yet exceptional side dish, it goes equally well alongside meat, fish, or poultry.

**SERVES 4**

  3  tablespoons olive oil

  1  large clove garlic, minced

  2  pounds carrots (about 16), cut diagonally into ½-inch slices

  1  teaspoon sugar

 ½  teaspoon salt

 ¼  teaspoon fresh-ground black pepper

  1  tablespoon chopped fresh marjoram, or 1 teaspoon dried marjoram

  4  teaspoons lemon juice

1. In a medium nonstick frying pan, heat 1½ tablespoons of the oil over moderately low heat. Add the garlic, carrots, sugar, ¼ teaspoon of the salt, the pepper, and the dried marjoram, if using. Cook, covered, stirring occasionally, for 5 minutes.

2. Uncover the pan. Raise the heat to moderate and cook, stirring frequently, until the carrots are very tender and beginning to brown, about 8 minutes longer.

3. Remove the pan from the heat. Stir in the remaining 1½ tablespoons oil and ¼ teaspoon salt, the lemon juice, and the fresh marjoram, if using.

# CHICKEN POTPIE

Marjoram isn't the only thing giving an old favorite a delicious new twist; the crust is made from buttery, golden-brown bread crumbs instead of time-consuming pie pastry.

**WINE RECOMMENDATION**
This satisfying potpie calls for a fairly full-bodied, substantial white wine, such as a chardonnay from California. A relatively light-bodied red, perhaps an inexpensive Beaujolais, could also complement the dish nicely.

**SERVES 4**

| | |
|---|---|
| 5 | tablespoons butter |
| 1 | onion, cut into thin slices |
| 3 | carrots, cut into thin slices |
| ¾ | pound mushrooms, cut into thin slices |
| ¾ | teaspoon salt |
| ¼ | teaspoon fresh-ground black pepper |
| 3½ | tablespoons flour |
| 1½ | cups canned low-sodium chicken broth or homemade stock |
| ½ | cup half-and-half or light cream |
| 1 | tablespoon chopped fresh marjoram, or 1 teaspoon dried marjoram |
| 1⅓ | pounds boneless, skinless chicken breasts (about 4 in all), cut into 1 inch cubes |
| 2 | cups fresh bread crumbs |

1. Heat the oven to 400°. In a 10- or 12-inch ovenproof frying pan or large saucepan, melt 3 tablespoons of the butter over moderate heat. Add the onion and carrots and cook, covered, stirring occasionally, until the onion is translucent, about 5 minutes. Add the mushrooms, ¼ teaspoon of the salt, and the pepper. Cook, covered, stirring occasionally, for 5 minutes longer.

2. Stir the flour into the vegetables. Whisk in the broth, half-and-half, marjoram, and the remaining ½ teaspoon salt. Bring to a simmer and continue simmering until the sauce starts to thicken, about 2 minutes. Remove from the heat and add the chicken. If using a saucepan, pour the mixture into an 8-by-12-inch baking dish.

3. In a medium saucepan, melt the remaining 2 tablespoons butter. Remove from the heat and stir in the bread crumbs. Sprinkle the buttered bread crumbs in an even layer over the chicken mixture. Bake in the oven until the crumbs begin to brown, 10 to 12 minutes.

MINT *The mint you're most likely to find at the supermarket, spearmint, is just one of over sixty varieties of the herb. Spearmint can be used interchangeably with its even bolder brother peppermint, though the latter is most often found in the form of peppermint oil and used as a flavoring for candies, desserts, and liqueurs. Other choices range from the milder basil and apple mints to the especially fruity pineapple mint to the most intense mint of all, lemon mint. For the fullest flavor from fresh mint, crush the leaves before using them. Dried mint is strong but lacks the true taste of fresh; use it if fresh is not available, but only in cooked dishes.* ❧ **USES** *Mint is a favorite the world over. It's found in Sicilian pasta dishes, in Indian chutneys and yogurt raitas, in Middle Eastern tabbouleh, in many Vietnamese specialties (where it's often paired with cilantro), and in Portuguese soups. Try also: making a traditional English sauce for lamb by steeping mint in vinegar; adding crushed sprigs to summer drinks such as iced tea and sangria; tossing chopped mint with peas, carrots, new potatoes, or fresh fruit; stirring it into sour cream along with some brown sugar and serving it over strawberries.*

# BERRIES WITH LEMON MINT SYRUP

Crushed mint leaves and strips of lemon peel are steeped in a sugar syrup, which is then tossed with fresh berries for a refreshingly light fruit compote. We've used the more readily available spearmint here, but if you happen on pineapple mint, by all means use it instead.

**SERVES 4**

1½  cups water

¾  cup sugar

1  cup firmly packed mint leaves and tender stems, crushed, plus 4 sprigs for garnish (optional), or ⅓ cup dried mint

Zest from 1 lemon, cut off in ½-inch-wide strips

1½  quarts mixed berries, such as blueberries, raspberries, blackberries, and quartered strawberries

1.  In a medium saucepan, combine the water, sugar, mint leaves and stems or dried mint, and lemon zest. Bring to a boil. Remove from the heat and let stand, covered, for 20 minutes. If using fresh mint, remove it and the lemon zest with a slotted spoon and discard. If using dried mint, strain the syrup.

2.  Bring the syrup back to a simmer. Remove from the heat and add the berries. Stir gently and then pour into a bowl. Let cool to room temperature. Serve the berries and syrup in bowls topped with the fresh mint sprigs, if using.

# MINT TEA

Hot mint tea is a favorite in Morocco, where it's served in small glasses any time of day or night. It's very sweet and packed with mint flavor. We love it cold as well; let the tea cool completely and then strain it into ice-filled glasses.

**SERVES 4**

1 quart boiling water, plus more for heating the teapot

1 tablespoon loose green tea, or 3 bags green tea

¾ cup sugar

3 cups firmly packed mint leaves and tender stems, crushed, plus 4 sprigs for garnish

1. Pour a little boiling water into a large teapot, swish it around to heat the pot, and pour the water out. Add the tea to the teapot and pour in 1 cup of the boiling water. Cover and let steep 3 minutes.

2. Add the sugar and mint leaves and stems to the teapot. Pour in the remaining 3 cups boiling water. Cover and let steep for 5 minutes. Stir. Continue to steep for 5 minutes more. Strain the mint tea into cups or heatproof glasses.

# PIMM'S CUP

*The* drink to order at polo matches, this fruity concoction gets its name and its alcohol content from Pimm's No. 1, a British spirit. You can find it at any well-stocked liquor store.

**SERVES 4**

1½ cups Pimm's No. 1

1 navel orange, cut crosswise into thin slices

1 lemon, cut crosswise into thin slices

¾ cup firmly packed mint leaves and tender stems

1½ cups cold ginger ale or lemon lime soda

1 cucumber, cut lengthwise into 8 wedges

About 3 cups ice

1 apple, quartered, cored, and cut into thin slices

1. In a large pitcher, combine the Pimm's, the orange and lemon slices, and the mint. Chill for about 10 minutes. Stir in the ginger ale.

2. Put two cucumber wedges, standing on end, into each of four 1-pint glasses. Fill halfway with ice. Pour in the Pimm's mixture. Push the mint down into the drinks and divide the orange, lemon, and apple slices among the drinks.

# PENNE WITH SWORDFISH, MINT, AND PINE NUTS

In this Sicilian dish, pasta, pine nuts, and chunks of swordfish are tossed in mint-spiked olive oil, with more fresh mint thrown in at the end. The combination is irresistible.

**WINE RECOMMENDATION**
Although a meaty fish such as swordfish can usually take a red wine, the minty accents here are better accentuated by a crisp white wine such as a pinot grigio from Italy or a sauvignon blanc from Washington State.

**SERVES 4**

¼  cup pine nuts

¼  cup plus ½ tablespoon olive oil

1  pound swordfish steak, about 1 inch thick

¾  teaspoon salt

¼  teaspoon fresh-ground black pepper

3  cloves garlic, minced

½  cup chopped fresh mint

¾  pound penne

1. In a small frying pan, toast the pine nuts over moderately low heat, stirring frequently, until golden brown, about 5 minutes. Or toast them in a 350° oven for 5 to 10 minutes.

2. In a large nonstick frying pan, heat the ½ tablespoon oil over moderate heat. Sprinkle the swordfish with ¼ teaspoon of the salt and the pepper. Add the fish to the pan and cook 4 minutes. Turn and cook until the fish is just done, 2 to 3 minutes longer. Remove. When the fish is cool enough to handle, cut it into 1-inch cubes.

3. Wipe out the pan. Add the remaining ¼ cup oil to the pan and heat over moderately low heat. Add the garlic and cook, stirring, for 1 minute. Stir in ¼ cup of the mint and remove the pan from the heat.

4. In a large pot of boiling, salted water, cook the penne until just done, about 13 minutes. Drain and toss with the swordfish, the garlic-and-mint oil, the pine nuts, the remaining ¼ cup mint, and ½ teaspoon salt.

## VARIATION

You can use **tuna** in place of the swordfish. Cook the tuna a few minutes less than the swordfish so that it's still pink inside.

**OREGANO** *No fragile flavors here—oregano makes its presence known with a pungent, peppery kick. Not only does it dry well, but many cooks feel the flavor actually improves as the leaves dry. Both fresh and dried oregano appear frequently in Italian, Greek, and Mexican kitchens. The Mexican variety of the herb is even stronger than the Mediterranean, so add a healthy dose of supermarket dried oregano to south-of-the-border dishes. Dried oregano is often substituted for marjoram, which does not dry as well.* 🌿 **USES** *Oregano is the quintessential pizza herb and, in fact, is a welcome addition to any dish featuring both tomatoes and cheese. You'll find it frequently in spaghetti sauce and chili. It shines, too, when combined with chopped garlic and grated lemon zest; enjoy this combination sprinkled over roasted chicken, fried potatoes, or grilled pork. Try also: marinating red snapper with garlic, lime juice, and oregano before roasting or grilling it; tossing a little oregano into fresh tomato salsa; stirring some oregano into sautéed zucchini or mushrooms; pushing fresh leaves of the herb between the skin and meat of a chicken before roasting for a pretty and toothsome effect.*

# STEAK PIZZAIOLA

In Italy, the briefly cooked fresh tomato sauce called *pizzaiola* is traditionally served atop steak. We use sirloin, but if you'd prefer to use flank steak or skirt steak, just reduce the cooking time. The sauce is also good on pasta.

**WINE RECOMMENDATION**
Barbera—a dry, crisp, medium-bodied red wine from northwestern Italy—is ideal whenever tomatoes and beef come together.

**SERVES 4**

- 4 tablespoons olive oil, plus more if needed
- 2 cloves garlic, minced
- 1½ pounds tomatoes (about 3), peeled and chopped
- 3 sprigs plus ½ teaspoon chopped fresh oregano, or ¾ teaspoon dried oregano
- ¾ teaspoon salt
- ½ teaspoon fresh-ground black pepper
- 1½ pounds sirloin steak, about 1 inch thick

1. In a large saucepan, heat 2 tablespoons of the oil over moderate heat. Add the garlic and cook, stirring, for 1 minute. Add the tomatoes, oregano sprigs or dried oregano, ½ teaspoon of the salt, and ¼ teaspoon of the pepper. Reduce the heat and simmer, partially covered, until the sauce thickens, about 15 minutes.

2. In a large frying pan, heat the remaining 2 tablespoons oil over moderate heat. Season the steak with the remaining ¼ teaspoon salt and ¼ teaspoon pepper. Cook the steak for 5 minutes. Turn and cook until done to your taste, about 5 minutes longer for medium rare. Remove the steak and let rest in a warm spot for 5 minutes. Cut the steak diagonally into thin slices and top with the warm tomato sauce and the chopped fresh oregano, if using.

# MEXICAN MEATBALL SOUP

Studded with zucchini, corn, and tomatoes, our brothy soup is comforting, especially on chilly evenings. Oregano flavors both the liquid and the meatballs.

**WINE RECOMMENDATION**
The oregano, jalapeños, and cumin here would give most wines a run for their money, but a lusty red zinfandel is spicy and rich enough to face those powerful ingredients without flinching.

**SERVES 4**

1 tablespoon cooking oil

1 small red onion, chopped

2 jalapeño peppers, seeds and ribs removed, chopped

1 zucchini (about ½ pound), cut into ½-inch dice

2¼ teaspoons dried oregano, or 2 tablespoons chopped fresh oregano

½ teaspoon ground cumin

1 quart canned low-sodium chicken broth or homemade stock

2 cups water

1½ cups drained canned diced tomatoes (one 15-ounce can)

1¾ teaspoons salt

¾ teaspoon fresh-ground black pepper

½ pound ground beef

2 cloves garlic, minced

2½ tablespoons dry bread crumbs

1 egg, beaten to mix

1 cup fresh (cut from about 2 ears) or frozen corn kernels

1 tablespoon lime juice

1. In a large pot, heat the oil over moderately low heat. Add the onion and half the jalapeños and cook, stirring occasionally, until the onion is translucent, about 5 minutes. Add the zucchini, 1½ teaspoons of the dried oregano, if using, and ¼ teaspoon of the cumin and cook, stirring, until the zucchini starts to soften, about 3 minutes.

2. Add the broth, water, tomatoes, 1¼ teaspoons of the salt, and ½ teaspoon of the black pepper; bring to a simmer. Simmer for 15 minutes.

3. Meanwhile, in a medium bowl, combine the ground beef, garlic, the remaining jalapeño, ¼ teaspoon cumin, ¾ teaspoon dried oregano or 1 tablespoon of the fresh oregano, ½ teaspoon salt, and ¼ teaspoon black pepper, the bread crumbs, and the egg. Shape the mixture into 24 meatballs, about 1 inch in diameter.

4. Add the meatballs and corn to the soup and simmer until the meatballs are just done, about 5 minutes. Stir in the lime juice and the remaining 1 tablespoon fresh oregano, if using.

PARSLEY *It's time to give parsley its due. Long left to languish at the edge of plates as a garnish, parsley is both flavorful enough to be considered an important herb and versatile enough to be a constant presence in your refrigerator. It doesn't hurt that both varieties—curly and flat-leaf—are cheap and readily available. Though flat-leaf has long been the darling of the food cognoscenti, the flavor of curly parsley can be equally good. Use only fresh parsley, and be sure to wash the leaves well to remove the grit before adding them to a dish. After chopping the leaves, don't throw away the stems; they're the most flavorful part and make a worthy addition to the stockpot. You can also chew them as a breath freshener.* 🌿 **USES** *With parsley, you have virtually unlimited options. It goes with just about everything. The herb is the base of sauces like spicy chimichurri. It's classic in the versatile combination fines herbes and, with lemon juice, in maître d'hôtel butter. Try also: deep-frying curly-parsley leaves as a tempting garnish for fish; tossing whole leaves with the lettuce in a salad; adding parsley to any mushroom dish; stirring chopped parsley into scrambled eggs.*

# PARSLEY SALAD

Parsley rather than lettuce acts as the base for an unusual and hearty salad. Mushrooms, cherry tomatoes, scallions, and pine nuts make this an interesting mix indeed. Be sure to use curly parsley. The flat variety won't stand up to the dressing; the leaves get plastered together rather than combining nicely with the other ingredients.

**SERVES 4**

- ¼ cup pine nuts
- 1 tablespoon wine vinegar
- 1 teaspoon Dijon mustard
- ½ teaspoon salt
- ⅛ teaspoon fresh-ground black pepper
- ¼ cup olive oil
- 1½ quarts lightly packed curly-parsley leaves
- 2 scallions including green tops, cut into thin slices
- 1½ cups halved cherry tomatoes
- ¼ pound mushrooms, cut into thin slices

1. In a small frying pan, toast the pine nuts over moderately low heat, stirring frequently, until golden brown, about 5 minutes. Or toast them in a 350° oven for 5 to 10 minutes.

2. In a large glass or stainless-steel bowl, whisk together the vinegar, mustard, salt, and pepper. Add the oil slowly, whisking.

3. Add the parsley, scallions, tomatoes, and mushrooms and toss. Top with the pine nuts.

# CATFISH AND POTATOES WITH SALSA VERDE

Salsa verde—the parsley and caper sauce traditionally served with meat and fish—adds a welcome kick to potatoes, too. In season, sliced tomatoes will also benefit from the sauce. Add them to the plate, and you'll have a complete meal.

**WINE RECOMMENDATION**
Once one of the most popular of all Italian whites, Verdicchio is better than ever these days. Sip it with this dish and discover how the wine's tangy character complements both fish and pungent sauces.

**SERVES 4**

²/₃ cup lightly packed flat-leaf parsley leaves

3 tablespoons drained capers

1 clove garlic

4 teaspoons lemon juice

1 teaspoon anchovy paste

½ teaspoon Dijon mustard

¾ teaspoon salt

Fresh-ground black pepper

8 tablespoons olive oil

1 pound small new potatoes (about 6), quartered, or boiling potatoes (about 3), cut into 1-inch chunks

4 catfish fillets, about ½ inch thick (about 2 pounds in all)

1. Put the parsley, capers, garlic, lemon juice, anchovy paste, mustard, ¼ teaspoon of the salt and ⅛ teaspoon pepper in a blender. Pulse to chop.

With the machine running, add 7 tablespoons of the oil in a thin stream to make a smooth puree.

2. Put the potatoes in a medium saucepan of salted water. Bring to a boil, reduce the heat, and simmer until tender, about 15 minutes. Drain.

3. Light the grill or heat the broiler. Coat the fish with the remaining 1 tablespoon oil and sprinkle with the remaining ½ teaspoon salt and ¼ teaspoon pepper. Grill or broil the fish for 3 minutes. Turn and cook until just done, 3 to 4 minutes longer.

4. To serve, drizzle some of the salsa verde over the fish and potatoes. Serve the remaining salsa verde alongside.

## FISH ALTERNATIVES

In place of the catfish, you can use **swordfish**, **salmon**, **halibut**, or **tuna steaks**, or **mahimahi** or **mackerel fillets**—really almost any fish you can grill.

# VEAL CHOPS WITH GREMOLADA

You'll find that gremolada—the flavor-packed combination of parsley, garlic, and lemon zest most familiar as the final touch on ossobuco—brings simple sautéed veal chops to life.

**WINE RECOMMENDATION**
Any crisp, dry white wine can accompany the veal nicely; however, a good-quality Soave will be ideal with the gremolada.

**SERVES 4**

3   tablespoons chopped fresh parsley

Grated zest from 1 lemon

1   clove garlic, minced

3   tablespoons olive oil

4   veal loin chops, about 1 inch thick (about 3 pounds in all)

1/2   teaspoon salt

1/4   teaspoon fresh-ground black pepper

1. In a small bowl, combine the parsley, lemon zest, and garlic.

2. In a large nonstick frying pan, heat the oil over moderate heat. Sprinkle the chops with the salt and pepper. Cook the chops until just done, about 5 minutes per side. Serve the chops topped with the gremolada.

## GREGARIOUS GREMOLADA

A sprinkling of gremolada will not only get along with but will improve meat, fish, poultry, and vegetables, too. Try it on lamb or pork chops, steaks, sautéed chicken, fish fillets, scallops or shrimp, potatoes, asparagus—the list is endless.

**ROSEMARY** *Rosemary is powerful. The herb has a strong scent, reminiscent of pine needles and camphor, and an equally strong flavor that's much more appealing than the elements of the aroma sound. As befits their strong smell and taste, the leaves of the rosemary bush are on the brawny side, too—tough, spiky, and not particularly palatable. You'll want to add rosemary leaves, particularly the dried ones, early in the cooking process to give them time to soften, or else chop the fresh leaves very fine.* 🌿 **USES** *Rosemary goes especially well with lamb. Sprinkle it on a rack or leg before grilling or roasting, or use it to flavor any sautéed or braised lamb dish. Don't make this an exclusive relationship, though; the herb is also harmoniously paired with pork and chicken and is delicious grilled with full-flavored fish such as tuna and bluefish. Try also: adding a sprig of rosemary to bean or lentil soups; simmering it in tomato soups and sauces; making rosemary-studded breads like focaccia; using it to flavor such desserts as pound cake and sorbet; infusing rosemary in oil, vinegar, or syrups to poach apples or pears.*

# LEMON AND ROSEMARY GRANITA

An icy treat for a warm summer evening, this granita gets an unexpected boost from the bold flavor of rosemary. You can put the hot lemon mixture directly into the freezer rather than chilling it first, but the freezing time will be longer.

**MAKES ABOUT 1 QUART GRANITA**

- 3 cups water
- 1 cup plus 2 tablespoons sugar
- 4 4-inch sprigs fresh rosemary, or 3 tablespoons dried rosemary, crumbled
- 4 $\frac{1}{2}$-by-3-inch strips lemon zest
- 1$\frac{1}{4}$ cups lemon juice (from about 5 lemons)
- 3 tablespoons Grand Marnier or other orange liqueur

1. In a medium saucepan, combine the water, sugar, rosemary, and lemon zest. Bring to a simmer, stirring occasionally. Remove from the heat, cover, and let infuse for 10 minutes.

2. In a large glass or stainless-steel bowl, combine the lemon juice and Grand Marnier. Strain the rosemary syrup into the lemon juice and stir to combine. Chill in the refrigerator or, to hasten the process, pour the lemon mixture into a stainless-steel bowl, set it in a larger bowl filled with ice, and stir until cold.

3. Pour the chilled lemon mixture into two 9-by-9-inch stainless-steel pans. Freeze for 15 minutes. Stir well and return the pans to the freezer. Continue freezing, stirring every 15 minutes, until the granita is completely frozen, about 1 hour in all. When ready to serve, scoop the granita into chilled bowls or stemmed glasses.

# LAMB CHOPS WITH ROSEMARY AND GRAPES

You'd expect to find lamb chops grilled with rosemary, but the sauce, a fruity mixture of grapes, white wine, and just a touch of honey, is a delightful surprise. You'll want to choose seedless grapes for this recipe.

 **WINE RECOMMENDATION**
Cabernet sauvignon is classic with lamb, but a European cabernet will taste austere against the slightly sweet sauce here. Instead, try a California or Washington State cabernet, which will be fruity enough to blend with the sweetness.

**SERVES 4**

1½    tablespoons olive oil

8    lamb loin chops, about 1¼ inches thick (about 3 pounds in all)

Salt

Fresh-ground black pepper

3    tablespoons chopped fresh rosemary

4    cloves garlic, cut into thin slices

2    cups red grapes (from about a 1-pound bunch)

⅓    cup dry white wine

1    teaspoon honey

1. In a large stainless-steel or nonstick frying pan, heat the oil over moderately high heat. Season the lamb chops with ½ teaspoon salt and ¼ teaspoon pepper. Put the chops in the pan and sprinkle 1½ tablespoons of the rosemary in the spaces between the chops. Cook the chops for 5 minutes. Turn and sprinkle the garlic in between the chops. Cook the chops until done to your taste, 3 to 5 minutes longer for medium rare.

2. Remove the chops and garlic and keep in a warm spot. Pour off all but 2 tablespoons of the fat from the pan. Add the grapes and the remaining 1½ tablespoons rosemary to the pan. Reduce the heat and cook, stirring frequently, until the grapes soften, about 8 minutes.

3. Add the wine to the pan and simmer 2 minutes. Stir in the garlic and any juices from the lamb, the honey, ⅛ teaspoon salt, and a pinch of pepper. Serve the lamb topped with the grapes and sauce.

---

### VARIATION

In place of the loin chops, you can use **lamb shoulder chops**, about one inch thick (about two pounds in all). Cook them a little less than the loin chops.

---

**SAGE** *Once limited to stuffing for the holiday bird, sage has come into its own. Credit can go largely to the renaissance in America of Italian regional cooking, which makes good and frequent use of sage. The herb's flavor is undeniably strong, almost musty, yet can enhance even the most delicate of dishes. Stronger still is dried sage; use it sparingly. Though the herb comes in many, many decorative varieties, the two commonly used for cooking are narrow-leaved and broad-leaved sage.* **USES** *Sage is a key ingredient in sausages and, in fact, is delicious with any rich meat or poultry, such as pork or goose. At the other extreme, sage has a great affinity for delicate trout. It's a classic with cannellini beans and delicious with both tomatoes and cheese. Try also: sautéing sage leaves in brown butter to top ravioli, fish, veal cutlets, or even cauliflower; combining chopped sage with prosciutto and fontina cheese as a stuffing for chicken breasts or pork chops; tossing chunks of winter squash with sage and olive oil and then roasting; putting sage leaves under the skin of a chicken before roasting; steeping the leaves in warm water for an interesting herbal tisane.*

# GRILLED FONTINA, MUSHROOM, AND SAGE SANDWICHES

The grilled cheese sandwich grows up in our sophisticated version that starts with nutty, smooth-melting fontina cheese and adds a layer of sage-accented sautéed mushrooms.

**WINE RECOMMENDATION**
A crisp, dry, Italian white—such as Soave, Frascati, or pinot grigio—will refresh your mouth after every bite of this flavorful sandwich.

**SERVES 4**

3 tablespoons butter, 2 melted

½ pound mushrooms, cut into thin slices

¼ teaspoon salt

⅛ teaspoon fresh-ground black pepper

4 teaspoons chopped fresh sage, or 1¼ teaspoons dried sage

8 slices from a large round loaf of country-style bread, or other bread

½ pound fontina, grated (about 2 cups)

1. In a large nonstick frying pan, heat 1 tablespoon of the butter over moderate heat. Add the mushrooms, salt, pepper, and dried sage, if using, and cook, stirring frequently, until golden brown, about 5 minutes. Stir in the fresh sage, if using. Put the mushrooms in a bowl and wipe out the pan.

2. Using a pastry brush, coat one side of 4 slices of the bread with half of the melted butter. Put them, buttered-side down, on a work surface. Top the bread with the cheese and then the mushrooms. Cover with the remaining 4 slices of bread; brush the tops with the remaining melted butter.

3. Heat the frying pan over moderately low heat. Add the sandwiches and cook, turning once, until golden, about 5 to 10 minutes per side.

# Pumpkin Soup with Sage and Ham

Sage and pumpkin are a perfect pair. Add chunks of apple and ham and you have the makings of a delicious autumn soup. We use canned pumpkin here in the name of speed, but in fact it tastes as good as fresh once it simmers with the vegetables and herbs. If the soup gets too thick, just stir in a little extra broth or water.

**WINE RECOMMENDATION**
Let a cool sauvignon blanc or fumé blanc from California bring its own combination of fruit and herbal flavors into play with the apple and sage of the soup.

**SERVES 4**

- 3 tablespoons butter
- 1 onion, chopped
- 1 carrot, chopped
- 1 rib celery, chopped
- 1/2 tart apple, such as Granny Smith, peeled, cored, and cut into 1/2-inch dice
- 2 cups canned pumpkin puree (from one 16-ounce can)
- 1/3 cup dry white wine
- 1 tablespoon dried sage
- 1 bay leaf
- 3 1/2 cups water
- 2 1/2 cups canned low-sodium chicken broth or homemade stock
- 1 1/2 teaspoons salt
- 1/4 teaspoon fresh-ground black pepper
- 1 1/2-pound piece of ham, cut into 1/4-inch dice

1. In a large pot, melt the butter over moderate heat. Add the onion, carrot, celery, and apple and cook, stirring occasionally, until the onion is translucent, about 10 minutes.

2. Stir in the pumpkin puree, wine, sage, and bay leaf. Add the water, broth, salt, and pepper and bring to a simmer. Reduce the heat and simmer, partially covered, for 15 minutes. Add the ham and simmer, uncovered, until the vegetables are tender, about 5 minutes longer. Remove the bay leaf.

 The well-earned title "bean herb" has been conferred on savory because it is such a perfect comple-ment to lentils, chickpeas, and fresh and dried beans of all kinds. The two main varieties, summer savory and winter savory, are actually different plants: summer is an annual, winter a perennial. Their flavors are similar, and although they're of differing strengths—winter is pungent and peppery, while summer is somewhat weaker—the contrast is not so great that you can't substitute one for the other with a little adjusting of quantities. Both varieties dry well, losing very little of their flavor. **USES** Savory has been used as everything from an aphrodisiac to a disinfectant, but it's most valued for the piquant, thymelike taste it brings to food. In addition to beans, savory tastes especially good with strong brassica veg-etables, such as Brussels sprouts and cabbage. It often shows up in sausages, stuffing, and even barbecue sauce. Try also: mix-ing some chopped fresh savory with butter to top a baked potato; sprinkling fresh savory and olive oil over goat cheese; sautéing corn kernels with onion and savory; marinating pork chops with savory before grilling; tossing it with roasted turnips.

# GRILLED TROUT WITH SAVORY MARINADE

Trout and summer savory form an ideal marriage. Both are mild-mannered, so they blend beautifully, neither upstaging the other. Serve the dish with equally mellow vegetables, such as buttered green beans and grilled or roasted potatoes.

**WINE RECOMMENDATION**
A delicately flavored Muscadet or Sancerre will enhance the trout rather than compete with it, and neither of these wines will be washed out by the lemon, because they are both high in acidity.

**SERVES 4**

4 teaspoons lemon juice

2½ teaspoons dried summer savory, or
    2½ tablespoons chopped fresh savory

¾ teaspoon salt

¼ teaspoon fresh-ground black pepper

⅓ cup olive oil

8 trout fillets (about 2 pounds in all)
    Lemon wedges, for serving

1. Light the grill or heat the broiler. In a small glass or stainless-steel bowl, whisk together the lemon juice, savory, salt, and pepper. Add the oil slowly, whisking.

2. Put the trout fillets in a medium glass dish or stainless-steel pan. Add the marinade and turn the fillets to coat.

3. Grill or broil the fish 2 minutes. Turn and cook until just done, about 2 minutes longer for ¼-inch-thick fillets. Serve with the lemon wedges.

# LENTIL SOUP WITH SMOKED SAUSAGE

This hearty soup, with its lentils and sausage, seems made for savory. For a special version, use imported Vertes du Puy lentils, which have a rich, earthy flavor. A firm whole-grain bread would be ideal alongside.

**WINE RECOMMENDATION**
The inexpensive red wines called *Côtes-du-Rhône*—from a district of the same name in the south of France—tend to have earthy and spicy flavors that will nicely balance those of the lentils and sausages.

**SERVES 4**

2   tablespoons cooking oil

2   ribs celery, chopped

1   large onion, chopped

1   carrot, chopped

1   pound lentils (about 2⅓ cups)

1½  cups drained canned diced tomatoes (one 15-ounce can)

2½  quarts water, more if needed

4   teaspoons dried summer savory, or ¼ cup chopped fresh savory

1   bay leaf

1¾  teaspoons salt

¼   teaspoon fresh-ground black pepper

½   pound kielbasa or other smoked sausage

1. In a large pot, heat the oil over moderate heat. Add the celery, onion, and carrot and cook, stirring occasionally, until the onion is translucent, 5 to 10 minutes.

2. Add the lentils, tomatoes, water, dried savory, if using, bay leaf, salt, and pepper. Bring to a simmer. Reduce the heat and cook, partially covered, until the lentils are tender, about 40 minutes.

3. Meanwhile, heat a large nonstick frying pan over moderately high heat. Add the sausage and cook, turning, until browned, about 3 minutes in all. Remove. When the sausage is cool enough to handle, cut it crosswise into ¼-inch-thick slices.

4. Stir the sausage and fresh savory, if using, into the soup and simmer it for 5 minutes longer. Remove the bay leaf. If the soup is too thick for your taste, thin it with additional water.

**TARRAGON** *So distinct is the aniselike flavor of tarragon that you must choose its herb partners with care. It's perfect in the classic blend of fines herbes—along with parsley, chervil, and chives—but completely at odds with stronger herbs such as rosemary and sage. A native of Russia, tarragon attained its greatest culinary value and recognition in France. You'll want to choose French tarragon over Russian tarragon, as the latter is nearly tasteless. Dried tarragon has a stronger flavor than fresh, but it will taste just like straw if left to sit too long on the shelf; replenish your supply often. Preserving tarragon in vinegar is another option. The herb loses its green color but still has lots of flavor, and the vinegar makes a delicious vinaigrette. Fresh tarragon fades quickly during cooking, so add it toward the end.*

**USES** *With its affinity for eggs, tarragon has an honored presence in such classic French creations as* oeufs en gelée, omelet aux fines herbes, *and* béarnaise sauce. *Another French favorite,* poulet à l'estragon, *shows off its way with chicken. Try also: using tarragon with fish and shellfish, peas, potatoes, mushrooms, and spinach.*

# SCALLOPS WITH TARRAGON BUTTER SAUCE

You can't go wrong with scallops in a white-wine butter sauce, and tarragon makes it all the better. Be careful not to heat the sauce too much or it may separate.

**WINE RECOMMENDATION**
For an extra dimension of flavor with this classic shellfish dish, try a pinot gris. Exciting examples are now coming out of Oregon.

**SERVES 4**

- 2 tablespoons olive oil
- 5 tablespoons butter
- 1½ pounds sea scallops, dried well
- 1 teaspoon salt
- ¼ teaspoon fresh-ground black pepper
- ⅓ cup dry white wine
- Grated zest of 1 lemon
- 2 tablespoons chopped fresh tarragon

1. In a large nonstick frying pan, heat 1 tablespoon of the oil with ½ tablespoon of the butter over moderate heat. Season the scallops with ½ teaspoon of the salt and the pepper. Put half the scallops in the pan. Cook until browned, about 2 minutes. Turn and cook until browned on the second side and just done, 1 to 2 minutes. Remove. Heat the remaining 1 tablespoon oil with ½ tablespoon of the butter in the pan and cook the remaining scallops. Remove.

2. Wipe out the pan. Put the pan over moderately low heat and add the wine. Boil until reduced to approximately 2 tablespoons, 1 to 2 minutes. Reduce the heat to the lowest setting. Whisk the remaining 4 tablespoons butter into the wine. The butter should not melt completely but just soften to form a smooth sauce. Add the remaining ½ teaspoon salt, the lemon zest, and the tarragon. Pour the sauce over the scallops.

# Spinach, Feta, and Tarragon Frittata

The combination of flavors here is pure genius. Tarragon is classic with both spinach and eggs, and a touch of sharp feta cheese accents the trio beautifully. Use these same ingredients to make superb omelets.

**WINE RECOMMENDATION**
Sparkling wines are perfect for egg dishes, especially eggs with cheese. A bottle of cava, Spain's classic and affordable bubbly, will turn a quick dish into a special occasion.

**SERVES 4**

2  tablespoons butter

2  scallions including green tops, cut into thin slices

10  ounces spinach, stems removed, leaves washed and cut into thin strips

1½  teaspoons dried tarragon, or 1½ tablespoons chopped fresh tarragon

¼  teaspoon salt

¼  teaspoon fresh-ground black pepper

8  large eggs

1  tablespoon olive oil

3  ounces feta, crumbled (about ⅓ cup)

1. In a 12-inch ovenproof nonstick frying pan, melt 1 tablespoon of the butter over moderate heat. Add the scallions and cook, stirring, for 1 minute. Add the spinach, dried tarragon, if using, and ⅛ teaspoon each of the salt and pepper. Cook, stirring frequently, until the liquid evaporates, about 3 minutes. Remove the spinach mixture and let cool. Wipe out the pan.

2. In a large bowl, beat the eggs with the remaining ⅛ teaspoon each salt and pepper. Stir in the spinach mixture and fresh tarragon, if using.

3. Heat the broiler. In the same frying pan, melt the remaining 1 tablespoon butter with the oil over moderate heat. Pour in the egg mixture and reduce the heat to low. Sprinkle the feta over the top and cook until the bottom is golden brown and the top is almost set, 6 to 7 minutes. Broil the frittata 6 inches from the heat, if possible, until the eggs are set, 2 to 3 minutes.

4. Lift up the edge of the frittata with a spatula and slide the frittata onto a plate. Cut into wedges and serve.

---

### TEST-KITCHEN TIP

If the handle of your frying pan isn't oven-proof, protect it from the heat of the broiler by wrapping it with about four layers of aluminum foil.

 **THYME** *Few herbs are as amenable as thyme. It gets along well with other herbs (even strong ones such as rosemary), is good fresh or dried, and improves the flavor of just about any dish. No wonder thyme occupies such an important place in European and North American cuisine. One of the most pleasing of all the Mediterranean herbs, thyme is a component of the famed French seasoning bouquet garni. There are over one hundred species of thyme, but the one you're most likely to encounter is garden thyme. Lemon thyme, a milder version with a citrus tang, is generally reserved for teas. When using fresh thyme, strip the leaves from the stems; you can then chop the leaves if you like, but they're small enough to use whole.* ❦ **USES** *It's hard to find any food that doesn't go well with thyme. Rice and other grains, dried beans, fish or shellfish, poultry, smoked or fresh meat, vegetables, fruit, and tomato or cream sauces—all these broad categories qualify as great matches. Try especially: adding thyme to lentil soup or lentil salad and to fresh tomato soup or sliced tomatoes; seasoning sautéed mushrooms or bell peppers with thyme; making a goat-cheese dip flavored with thyme; stirring thyme into rice pilaf.*

# SLICED ORANGES WITH THYME SYRUP

Oranges and thyme are magical together in this simple and elegant dessert. If you want a completely clear syrup without the bits of thyme, put the leaves in a tea ball and remove it once the syrup is chilled.

**SERVES 4**

1½ cups dry white wine

1½ cups water

¾ cup sugar

1 tablespoon fresh thyme leaves, or 1 teaspoon dried thyme

2 3-inch strips lemon zest

4 navel oranges

1. In a medium stainless-steel saucepan, combine the wine, water, sugar, thyme, and lemon zest. Bring to a simmer over moderately high heat. Reduce the heat and simmer for 10 minutes.

2. Meanwhile, using a stainless-steel knife, peel the oranges down to the flesh, removing all of the white pith. Cut the oranges crosswise into ¼-inch slices. Add the oranges to the simmering syrup. Remove from the heat and let sit 1 to 2 minutes. Gently pour the oranges and syrup into a glass or stainless-steel bowl. Let cool and then chill.

# Roasted Cod and Potatoes with Thyme

Fish and thyme are a traditional combination, and paired with golden brown roasted potatoes, they become a simple and superb dish. All you need is a salad to complete the meal.

**WINE RECOMMENDATION**
These earthy flavors beg for a vibrant white wine to provide contrast. Any white based on the sauvignon blanc grape—especially an unoaked type, such as a French Sancerre or Pouilly-Fumé, a sauvignon from northeast Italy, or a New Zealand sauvignon blanc—will be terrific.

**SERVES 4**

1½ pounds baking potatoes (about 3), cut lengthwise into 8 wedges, wedges cut crosswise in half

5 tablespoons olive oil

1 teaspoon salt

½ teaspoon fresh-ground black pepper

15 thyme sprigs plus 2½ teaspoons chopped fresh thyme, or 2 teaspoons dried thyme

1½ pounds cod fillets or steaks, about 1 inch thick

1. Heat the oven to 450°. In a large roasting pan, toss the potatoes with 3 tablespoons of the oil, ½ teaspoon of the salt, and ¼ teaspoon of the pepper. Scatter the thyme sprigs or 1½ teaspoons of the dried thyme on top. Roast the potatoes for 10 minutes. Stir and continue cooking for 10 minutes longer.

2. Meanwhile, coat the fish with the remaining 2 tablespoons oil and sprinkle the remaining ½ teaspoon salt, ¼ teaspoon pepper, and ½ teaspoon dried thyme or 1½ teaspoons of the chopped fresh thyme on the fish.

3. Remove the pan from the oven. Stir the potatoes and push them to one side of the pan. Put the fish on the other side of the pan and return the pan to the oven. Roast the fish and potatoes until just done, about 10 minutes longer.

4. Remove the fish. Toss the potatoes with the remaining 1 teaspoon chopped fresh thyme, if using. Serve the fish with the potatoes alongside.

---

## VARIATIONS

You can use other firm white fish fillets, such as **scrod**, **halibut**, or **haddock**, in place of the cod in this recipe.

---

# Spices

**ALLSPICE** *True to its name, allspice tastes like a mixture of cloves, cinnamon, and nutmeg, with a dash of black pepper. It grows in the form of berries that resemble peppercorns and are dried in the same way. In fact, adding a handful of allspice berries to your pepper mill along with the peppercorns makes an interesting variation on ground pepper. Though some recipes do require whole berries (for pickling and marinating) or crushed berries (with meats, poultry, and fish), ground allspice is the common form and the one called for most often.* ❊ **USES** *Allspice is a flavoring from the New World that is now used around the globe. It enhances vegetable and rice dishes and is a perfect all-purpose spice in desserts such as cakes, pies, puddings, and custards. Try also: using allspice in pâtés and sausage and with ham; tossing crushed allspice berries into shrimp or beef stir-fries; mixing the crushed berries with the black pepper for steak au poivre; adding ground allspice to sautéed carrots; making it part of a spice rub for pork; putting allspice in chutneys and relishes; letting it spice up applesauce, cheesecake, fruit quick breads, and butter cookies.*

# BAKED CUSTARD WITH ALLSPICE

Classic and homey baked custard benefits from a dusting of allspice instead of the usual nutmeg. Custards don't get much quicker to prepare than this one.

**SERVES 4**

2 cups milk

2 large eggs

2 large egg yolks

1/3 cup sugar

Pinch salt

1 teaspoon vanilla extract

1/4 teaspoon ground allspice

1. Heat the oven to 325°. Bring water to a simmer for the water bath. In a medium saucepan, bring the milk almost to a simmer, stirring occasionally.

2. In a medium bowl, whisk together the eggs, egg yolks, sugar, and salt until just combined. Pour the hot milk over the egg mixture, whisking. Stir in the vanilla. Strain the custard into a large measuring cup or pitcher and skim any foam from the surface.

3. Divide the custard among four 6-ounce custard cups or ramekins. Sprinkle the tops with the allspice and put them into a small roasting pan. Pour enough of the simmering water into the roasting pan to reach about halfway up the side of the custard cups. Carefully transfer the roasting pan to the middle of the oven and bake until a knife stuck in the center of the custard comes out clean, 45 minutes to 1 hour. Remove the cups from the water bath and let cool. Refrigerate until cold, at least 1 hour.

# CHICKEN-LIVER SALAD WITH HOT BACON DRESSING AND CROUTONS

Sprinkling allspice over chicken livers before sautéing adds a delicate spicy sweetness. With their smooth, rich texture, the livers are a pleasant contrast to the crisp bed of lettuce and crunchy croutons. Frisée stands up perfectly to the hot bacon dressing, but you can use another firm lettuce, such as curly endive, or a mixture of endive and radicchio, instead.

**WINE RECOMMENDATION**
Dishes that straddle the line between salad and meat need particularly flexible wines. Light-bodied reds that are low in tannin, to avoid a clash with the vinegar, can work well; try a Bardolino. Just about any dry rosé wine would also be good.

**SERVES 4**

1   ½-pound loaf country-style bread, crust removed, cut into ½-inch cubes (about 3 cups)

    About 7 tablespoons olive oil

2   large heads frisée, cut into 2-inch pieces (about 1½ quarts)

1   red onion, chopped

¾   teaspoon salt

    Fresh-ground black pepper

½   pound bacon, strips cut crosswise into ½-inch pieces

1   pound chicken livers, each cut in half

1   teaspoon ground allspice

3½  tablespoons wine vinegar

1. Heat the oven to 350°. Toss the bread cubes with 2 tablespoons of the oil and put on a large baking sheet. Bake, stirring once or twice, until the bread cubes are crisp and golden brown, about 15 minutes. Let the croutons cool.

2. In a large bowl, combine the frisée, onion, ½ teaspoon of the salt, and ¼ teaspoon pepper.

3. In a large nonstick frying pan, cook the bacon until crisp. Remove the bacon and pour the fat into a measuring cup. Add enough of the oil to make ½ cup and reserve for Step 5.

4. Wipe out the pan. Heat 1½ tablespoons of the oil in the pan over moderately high heat. Season the chicken livers with the allspice, the remaining ¼ teaspoon salt, and ⅛ teaspoon pepper. Put the livers in the pan, in two batches if necessary, and cook 2 minutes. Turn and cook until browned, about 2 minutes longer. The livers should still be pink inside. Remove the livers from the pan and put in a warm spot.

5. Wipe out the pan. Add the reserved ½ cup fat and the bacon to the pan. Heat over moderately high heat until the bacon is sizzling. Pour the hot bacon and fat over the salad and toss. Toss in the vinegar and then the croutons. Put the salad on plates and top with the livers.

**CARAWAY SEEDS** *Since the Stone Age, caraway has been used to flavor food. It became a popular part of Persian and Turkish cuisine before spreading to Europe and North America. These days, the spice is a particular favorite in Germany and Austria, where it is cooked with cabbage and potatoes. In northern Europe and in this country, however, it's probably best known for its presence in rye bread and other breads and rolls. This is the seed that gives the traditional English seed cake its name. Caraway is most familiar as whole seeds, but it's available ground. The mild and feathery leaves of fresh caraway, if you can find them, make a surprising herb. Try it almost anywhere you'd use parsley.* ❀ **USES** *In Tunisia, ground caraway and the whole seeds are used in combination with vegetables, salads, and couscous. Grind the seeds with garlic, sweet red peppers, chili peppers, and cilantro to make a paste called tabil, widely used in Tunisian cooking. Try also: adding caraway seeds to braised celery, sauerkraut, corned beef and cabbage, sautéed potatoes, hot potato salad, and sausages; sprinkling pork with ground caraway before roasting; using caraway in braised duck or goose dishes.*

# IRISH SODA LOAF

Caraway seeds are often included in Irish soda bread; they add a crunchy bite that contrasts with the sweet, soft raisins. Baking the bread as a rectangle in a loaf pan as opposed to the traditional round on a baking sheet preserves moistness and makes neat slices.

**MAKES ONE 9-INCH LOAF**

3¾  cups flour

½  cup sugar

4  teaspoons baking powder

½  teaspoon baking soda

½  teaspoon salt

¼  pound cold unsalted butter, cut into small cubes

1⅔  cups raisins

2  teaspoons caraway seeds

3  large eggs, at room temperature

1  cup buttermilk

1.  Heat the oven to 400°. Butter a 9-by-5-inch loaf pan. In a large bowl, whisk together the flour, sugar, baking powder, baking soda, and salt. Cut or rub in the butter until the mixture is the texture of fine meal. Stir in the raisins and caraway seeds.

2.  In a medium bowl, whisk two of the eggs to combine. Whisk in the buttermilk. Pour the buttermilk mixture into the dry ingredients and stir until just combined. Put the dough on a floured work surface, pat into a loaf, and put into the prepared pan. Beat the final egg to mix and brush the top of the loaf with it. Using a sharp knife, cut a ¼-inch-deep lengthwise slash down the middle of the loaf leaving a 1-inch margin at either end.

3.  Bake the soda bread in the middle of the oven until well browned and a toothpick inserted in the center comes out clean, 1 hour to 1 hour and 10 minutes. Turn the loaf out onto a rack and let cool. Serve warm or at room temperature.

# VEGETABLE COUSCOUS

Carrots, fennel, zucchini, and chickpeas in a broth spicy with jalapeños, caraway, and coriander make for a full-flavored vegetarian couscous. If you want to introduce meat, sautéed *merguez*—the hot North African sausages—are a great way to go.

**WINE RECOMMENDATION**
California chardonnays (and those from Washington State or Oregon) are earthy, rich, and slightly exotic—just like this dish. As you sip a chilled glass, the wine will also provide a cooling edge to the spice and heat of the food.

**SERVES 4**

¼ cup cooking oil

1 large onion, cut into thin slices

4 carrots, cut into thin slices

1 fennel bulb, cored and cut into 1-inch pieces

1 eggplant (about ¾ pound), cut into ½-inch pieces

4 cloves garlic, minced

1 jalapeño pepper, including seeds and ribs, cut diagonally into thin slices

¼ cup tomato paste

2 teaspoons ground coriander

1½ teaspoons caraway seeds

2¼ teaspoons salt

¼ teaspoon fresh-ground black pepper

5½ cups water

1⅔ cups drained and rinsed chickpeas (one 15-ounce can)

1⅓ cups couscous

1. In a large saucepan, heat the oil over moderate heat. Add the onion, carrots, fennel, eggplant, garlic, and jalapeño. Cook, covered, until the vegetables start to soften, about 10 minutes. Stir in the tomato paste, coriander, caraway seeds, 2 teaspoons of the salt, and the black pepper. Cook, stirring, for 1 minute.

2. Add 3½ cups of the water and bring to a boil. Reduce the heat and simmer, uncovered, until the vegetables are tender, about 15 minutes. Add the chickpeas and simmer 2 minutes longer.

3. Meanwhile, in a medium saucepan, bring the remaining 2 cups of water to a boil. Add the remaining ¼ teaspoon salt and the couscous. Cover. Remove the pot from the heat and let the couscous stand for 5 minutes. Fluff with a fork. Serve the stew with its broth over the couscous.

**CARDAMOM** *Berry-size cardamom pods are among the world's most expensive spices. The eucalyptus-tasting spice is most easily used either in its dried powdered form or as a crushed pod, which can be steeped in liquid or thrown into cooking food and then fished out before eating, like a bay leaf. Aficionados buy the pods, split them to release the seeds, and then grind the seeds. Choose green or white cardamom pods; the green have more flavor, though the white are really just green ones, bleached. Stay away from the larger brown cardamom pods; they are strong, but not pleasantly so.* ❀ **USES** *Cardamom shows up in everything from Indian curries to Middle Eastern coffees to Scandinavian cakes. Ground cardamom is delicious in sweet breads, muffins, and buttery cookies, and also complements fruit. Add a little to fruit salads, baked apples, or poached peaches or pears. Try also: infusing custard mixtures, custard sauces, and ice-cream bases with the pods; including them in the spice mixture for hot mulled wine; using the pods in spiced tea along with crushed fresh ginger and cinnamon sticks.*

# SHRIKHAND

Here's a classic Indian dessert, made with drained yogurt, cardamom, and saffron. The saffron is toasted until brittle so that you can grind it easily. If you grind your own cardamom seeds, use only a half teaspoon instead of the quantity in our recipe.

**SERVES 4**

Small pinch saffron

1 quart plain whole-milk yogurt

¾ teaspoon ground cardamom

2 tablespoons water

⅓ cup confectioners' sugar, or more to taste

¼ cup shredded coconut, unsweetened if possible

1 mango, cut into thin slices

1. In a small pan, toast the saffron over low heat, stirring, until brittle, about 2 minutes. Remove and pulverize in a mortar with a pestle or on a cutting board with the side of a large knife blade.

2. Put the yogurt in a large bowl. Put the saffron back into the pan and add the cardamom and water. Bring just to a simmer, stirring. Whisk the saffron mixture into the yogurt.

3. Put the yogurt mixture in a strainer lined with cheesecloth, a coffee filter, or a paper towel and set it over a bowl. Let drain in the refrigerator for 1 hour. Transfer the yogurt to a bowl. Add the ⅓ cup sugar, or more to taste. With an electric mixer, beat the yogurt until slightly thickened, 2 to 3 minutes. Pour into bowls and refrigerate until well chilled, or put in the freezer until very cold but not frozen, about 30 minutes.

4. Meanwhile, in a small frying pan, toast the coconut over low heat, stirring, until golden, about 2 minutes. Serve the *shrikhand* topped with the mango and coconut.

# CARDAMOM CHICKEN WITH RICE PILAF

Sprinkled with cardamom, roasted until crisp, and topped with an apple-flavored sauce, chicken legs become extraordinary. The chicken is perfectly matched by the raisin-studded rice pilaf that's also flavored with cardamom.

Raisins and apple juice contribute a slightly sweet fruitiness to this dish, contrasting with the cardamom. A California chardonnay that's oak aged—as most of them are—will provide a similar juxtaposition of sweet fruitiness and spice.

**SERVES 4**

|   |   |
|---|---|
| 4 | chicken legs (about 3 pounds) |
| 2½ | tablespoons cooking oil |
|   | Ground cardamom |
|   | Salt |
| ⅛ | teaspoon fresh-ground black pepper |
| 1 | tablespoon butter, cut into 4 pieces |
| 1 | small onion, minced |
| 1½ | cups basmati or other long-grain rice |
| ¼ | cup raisins |
| 2¼ | cups canned low-sodium chicken broth or homemade stock |
| ¼ | cup apple juice |

1. Heat the oven to 450°. Coat the chicken with 1 tablespoon of the oil and season with ½ teaspoon cardamom, ½ teaspoon salt, and the pepper. Put the chicken in a roasting pan and top each leg with a piece of the butter. Roast the chicken until just done, about 30 minutes.

2. Meanwhile, in a large saucepan, heat the remaining 1½ tablespoons oil over moderately low heat. Add the onion and cook, stirring occasionally, until translucent, about 5 minutes. Add the rice and 1 teaspoon cardamom and stir to coat the rice with the oil. Add the raisins, broth, and 1 teaspoon salt. Bring to a boil, reduce the heat to low and simmer, covered, for 20 minutes. Remove the pan from the heat and let sit, without removing the lid, for 5 minutes. Stir with a fork.

3. Remove the chicken from the pan. Pour off all the fat from the pan. Set the pan over the heat; add the apple juice and ⅛ teaspoon each cardamom and salt. Cook, scraping the bottom of the pan to dislodge any brown bits, until reduced to 2 tablespoons, about 3 minutes. Serve the chicken topped with a drizzle of the sauce and with the rice pilaf alongside.

## CELERY SEEDS

*A single tiny celery seed, about the size of the head of a pin, is enough to fill your whole mouth with the taste of celery. Add a few more, and you'll start to notice the seed's bitterness. Though it's quite handy for dishes where you want the flavor of celery but the vegetable would be out of place—biscuits, savory muffins, crackers—this is a spice you'll want to use sparingly. Many cooks cavalierly sprinkle the seeds anywhere that a touch of celery would be welcome, but you should first be sure the dish can withstand that bitter bite. Ground and mixed with salt, the seeds are also sold as celery salt.* ❀ **USES** *Celery seeds taste great with tomato juice; why not add a few to your Bloody Mary? The seeds complement eggs, fish, and many soups, too, and so make a tasty finishing touch for a fish chowder, either tomato or cream based. Try also: crushing the seeds and using them in a vinaigrette for chicken or tuna salad or mixed greens; adding them to cole slaw; making a frittata with potatoes, mozzarella, and celery seeds; simmering the seeds in the poaching liquid for salmon or other rich fish.*

# MUSSELS STEAMED IN TOMATO BROTH WITH GOAT CHEESE

Mussel and tomato juice and celery seeds make a delicious broth to accompany steamed mussels. Look for farmed mussels; they're clean, so you'll only have to scrub them briefly.

**WINE RECOMMENDATION**
Sancerre and Pouilly-Fumé, two white wines from the Loire Valley in France, are great with goat cheese and also have the acidity to make seafood taste even better.

**SERVES 4**

| | |
|---|---|
| 1½ | tablespoons cooking oil |
| 1 | small onion, chopped |
| 1½ | cups tomato juice |
| ½ | cup dry white wine |
| ¾ | teaspoon celery seeds |
| 4 | pounds mussels, scrubbed and debearded |
| 3 | ounces mild goat cheese, crumbled |

1. In a large pot, heat the oil over moderate heat. Add the onion. Cook, stirring occasionally, 3 minutes. Add the tomato juice, wine, and celery seeds; bring to a simmer. Cover; simmer 10 minutes.

2. Discard any mussels that are broken or do not clamp shut when tapped. Add the mussels to the pot. Cover and bring to a boil. Cook, shaking the pot occasionally, just until the mussels open, about 3 minutes. Remove the open mussels. Continue to boil, uncovering the pot as necessary to remove the mussels as soon as their shells open. Discard any that do not. Using a slotted spoon, put the mussels into four bowls.

3. Add the cheese to the broth and whisk over low heat for 1 minute. Pour over the mussels.

# STIR-FRIED PORK WITH CARROTS AND BOK CHOY

Celery isn't among the vegetables in this tasty pork stir-fry, but the celery seeds will make you think there's a generous quantity. Serve the stir-fry with steamed rice.

**WINE RECOMMENDATION**
Versatile pinot noir will have no problem handling the sweet-bitter accents of this dish.

**SERVES 4**

1½   pounds pork loin, cut into 1-inch cubes

1   teaspoon salt

¼   teaspoon fresh-ground black pepper

3   tablespoons cooking oil

1½   teaspoons cornstarch

1   tablespoon water

1   onion, cut into thin slices

3   carrots, cut into 2-inch-long slices about ½-inch wide and ⅛-inch thick

½   pound bok choy, cut into 1-inch pieces (about 3 cups)

2   cloves garlic, minced

½   teaspoon celery seeds

½   cup canned low-sodium chicken broth or homemade stock

¼   cup fresh orange juice

1.  In a medium bowl, toss the pork loin with ¼ teaspoon of the salt and the pepper. In a large frying pan or wok, heat 1 tablespoon of the oil over moderately high heat. Add half the pork and cook, stirring, until browned, 2 to 3 minutes.

Remove. Repeat with another tablespoon of the oil and the remaining pork. Remove.

2.  In a small bowl, combine the cornstarch and water. Heat the remaining 1 tablespoon oil in the pan. Add the onion, carrots, bok choy, garlic, and celery seeds. Cook, stirring, for 3 minutes. Stir in the broth and orange juice and bring to a simmer. Add the pork and any accumulated juices and the remaining ¾ teaspoon salt and simmer until the meat is just done, 1 to 2 minutes. Add the cornstarch mixture and cook, stirring, until the sauce thickens, about 1 minute.

## CINNAMON

*The familiar spice cinnamon comes from a laurel-like evergreen. The bark is stripped off the bush, the outer layer is planed off, and the remaining strips are dried into long, narrow rolls called cinnamon sticks. The sticks can be used whole or ground to a powder. Cassia, another bark sold in sticks, is sometimes mistaken for cinnamon, though real cinnamon is more delicate—and expensive.* ❄ **USES** *In the Middle East, cinnamon seasons meats such as lamb and poultry. In India, it flavors rice and meat dishes and is an important component of garam masala. But in America and throughout Europe, it's most often a dessert spice, appearing in cakes, puddings, pies, cookies, and anything with apples. Cinnamon's a particularly delicious addition to honey cake, carrot muffins, and pecan pie. Try also: putting ground cinnamon in pumpkin and squash soups and sweet-potato puree; rubbing the inside of a goose or duck with ground cinnamon; adding cinnamon sticks, along with bay leaves and cloves, to basmati rice before steaming it; infusing syrup, custard, and ice-cream bases with the sticks; including them in hot mulled wine or hot apple cider.*

# APPLE DUMPLINGS

Apples baked in flaky pastry with cinnamon sugar are irresistible, especially when served with vanilla ice cream. To save preparation time, we use frozen puff-pastry sheets.

**SERVES 4**

½  cup sugar

1  teaspoon ground cinnamon

2  frozen puff-pastry sheets (1 pound 1¼ ounces), thawed

1  egg, beaten to mix

4  Golden Delicious apples, peeled and cored

1.  Heat the oven to 425°. In a small bowl, combine the sugar and cinnamon. Set aside.

2.  On a floured surface, roll out one of the puff-pastry sheets to a 13-by-13-inch square. Cut the square in half and cut each half into a 9-by-6-inch rectangle. If you want to make the optional decoration in Step 3, reserve the scraps. With the beaten egg, lightly brush 1 inch along the edges of one of the rectangles. Put one of the apples, upside down, in the middle of the rectangle and pour enough of the cinnamon sugar into the center cavity to reach the top. Gather the four corners of the pastry and pinch them together. Pinch the edges together to seal. With scissors, trim any excess pastry from where the edges meet. Repeat with the remaining pastry, apples, and cinnamon sugar.

3.  If you like, use a small knife to cut eight small leaves from the scraps of pastry. Brush the backs of the leaves with the beaten egg and attach two of them to the top of each dumpling.

4.  Chill the dumplings for 15 minutes. Put them on a heavy baking sheet and lightly brush them with the beaten egg. Bake the dumplings for 8 minutes. Reduce the heat to 400° and continue cooking until golden, 20 to 22 minutes longer. Don't bake too long or the dumplings may burst.

# COUSCOUS-STUFFED CORNISH HENS

Moroccan-inspired couscous, chunky with apricots and almonds and flavored with cinnamon and honey, makes a quick and unexpected stuffing for roasted hens. The honey drizzled on the birds during the last ten minutes of cooking gives them a glistening, crisp, brown skin.

**WINE RECOMMENDATION**
This exotic dish calls for an equally exotic wine, like a delicious Australian sémillon—a not-too-dry white with hints of tangerine and almonds.

**SERVES 4**

¼ cup slivered almonds

½ cup canned low-sodium chicken broth or homemade stock

¼ cup dried apricots, chopped

Salt

½ cup couscous

1½ tablespoons butter

2½ teaspoons honey

¼ teaspoon ground cinnamon

Fresh-ground black pepper

2 Cornish hens (about 1¼ pounds each)

1 tablespoon cooking oil

3 tablespoons water

1. Heat the oven to 350°. Toast the nuts in the oven until golden brown, 5 to 10 minutes. Remove. Raise the heat to 425°.

2. In a small saucepan, bring the broth, the apricots, and ¼ teaspoon salt to a simmer over moderately high heat. Remove from the heat and stir in the couscous. Cover and let sit for 5 minutes. Fluff with a fork. Add the almonds, ½ tablespoon of the butter, 1½ teaspoons of the honey, the cinnamon, and ⅛ teaspoon each salt and pepper.

3. Fill the cavities of the hens with the couscous mixture. Twist the wings of the hens behind their backs and, if you like, tie the legs together. Put the hens, breast-side up, in a small roasting pan. Coat the hens with the oil; sprinkle with ⅛ teaspoon each salt and pepper. Dot with the remaining 1 tablespoon butter.

4. Roast the hens for 25 minutes. Baste them with the pan juices and drizzle with the remaining 1 teaspoon honey. Continue roasting until just done, 10 to 15 minutes longer.

5. When the hens are done, transfer them to a plate and leave to rest in a warm spot for about 5 minutes. Spoon the fat from the roasting pan and add the water to the juices. Cook over moderate heat, scraping the bottom of the pan to dislodge any brown bits, until reduced to ¼ cup, about 3 minutes. Add a pinch each of salt and pepper. Cut the hens in half and serve with the stuffing and pan juices.

 *The domineering clove has to be kept under control or it will overpower every flavor it comes near. Use it whole or ground, but use it sparingly. Heat tames the spice somewhat; it's rarely used uncooked. The name clove comes from the Latin clavus, or nail, and that's just what the whole spice looks like, tiny nails. They're really unopened flower buds from the tall evergreen clove tree that originated in the Spice Islands and is now grown in many areas of Southeast Asia.* ❧ **USES** *Ground cloves are an integral part of spice blends around the world, including Chinese five-spice powder, Indian garam masala, Western pickling spices, and Indonesian, West Indian, and Caribbean spice mixtures. The whole spice is used in European stocks and braised meat dishes such as daube and pot-au-feu. Try also: sprinkling ground cloves lightly over pork tenderloin before roasting; adding a pinch of ground cloves to winter squash; putting whole cloves in the syrup for poached fresh fruit, spiced peaches, or stewed fruit (cloves and prunes are a particularly felicitous match); using ground cloves in ice cream or butter cookies or in fruit desserts such as fruitcake or orange, lemon, or banana cake.*

# CRANBERRY APPLE RAISIN CRISP

We like to serve this homey dessert warm with vanilla ice cream. If you prefer it straight, reduce the amount of ground cloves to one-eighth teaspoon, or the flavor may be overwhelming. Be sure your baking dish is at least two inches deep so the sweet juices don't bubble over the edge and burn onto your oven floor. If the crisp comes to the top of the dish, put a baking sheet under it.

**SERVES 4**

- ½ cup old-fashioned oats
- ½ cup plus 2 tablespoons flour
- ½ cup dark brown sugar
- 5½ tablespoons cold butter, cut into ¼-inch pieces
- 1 12-ounce package cranberries (about 3 cups)
- 2 Golden Delicious apples, peeled, cored, and cut into ½-inch pieces
- ½ cup raisins
- ¾ cup granulated sugar
- Grated zest of 1 orange
- ½ cup orange juice (from about 1 orange)
- ¼ teaspoon ground cloves

1. Heat the oven to 375°. In a medium bowl, combine the oats, the ½ cup flour, and the brown sugar. Add the butter and rub it into the flour mixture until small crumbs form.

2. In a large bowl, combine the cranberries, apples, raisins, granulated sugar, the 2 tablespoons flour, orange zest and juice, and the cloves. Transfer the fruit to an 8-inch square glass baking dish or a 2-quart soufflé dish.

3. Top the fruit with the crumb mixture. Bake until the fruit is tender and the crumb topping has browned, about 45 minutes. Let cool at least 15 minutes before serving.

# SHRIMP BOIL

Eating a shrimp boil is fun and messy, with each person shelling his or her own shrimp at the table. We've given this Southern tradition a double dose of cloves and bay leaves, adding the whole spices to the ground ones already in the Old Bay Seasoning. The result is a deliciously spicy mound of shrimp, potatoes, and onion.

**WINE RECOMMENDATION**
The wine to best accompany this dish will be one that accommodates the intense flavors of the food rather than contributing distinctive flavors of its own. Verdicchio, an Italian white that's terrific with fish, will do just that.

**SERVES 4**

4 quarts water

6 cloves garlic, peeled

½ lemon, cut into 4 wedges

¼ cup Old Bay Seasoning

10 cloves

2 bay leaves

2 teaspoons salt

½ teaspoon Tabasco sauce

1 pound boiling potatoes (about 3), quartered

1 onion, cut through the root end into 8 wedges

1½ pounds large shrimp

1. In a large pot, bring the water, garlic, lemon, Old Bay Seasoning, cloves, bay leaves, salt, and Tabasco sauce to a boil. Reduce the heat and simmer for 10 minutes.

2. Add the potatoes and onion and simmer until both are tender, about 15 minutes.

3. Add the shrimp to the pot and bring back to a boil. Simmer until the shrimp are just done, about 1 minute. Using a slotted spoon, put the shrimp, onion, and potatoes onto a large, deep platter or into individual shallow bowls. Ladle some of the liquid over all.

## OLD BAY SEASONING

An unlikely combination that nevertheless tastes great with shellfish such as shrimp and crab, Old Bay Seasoning is a hot spice blend of celery salt, mustard, red pepper, black pepper, bay leaves, cloves, allspice, ginger, mace, cardamom, cinnamon, and paprika. It's sold in most supermarkets, but if you prefer to mix your own, start with the list above and combine them in amounts that suit your taste.

**CORIANDER** *The mild-mannered spice called coriander may come from the same plant as the herb cilantro (see page 37), but their flavors are nothing alike. While cilantro is pungent enough to stand out in a crowd, coriander is delicate, slightly citrusy, and a perfect companion for other spices. It is decidedly not interchangeable with the leafy green herb but adds subtle interest wherever it's used, whether whole, crushed into bits, or ground fine.* ❊ **USES** *Coriander is a welcome addition to both sweet and savory dishes. A versatile spice, it can be found in pickled foods, in hot dogs and mortadella, and in Indian curry powders. Coriander is good with many meats, especially lamb and pork; rub some on chops before grilling or sautéing. Its flavor blends well with garlic, chiles, dried beans, and vegetables such as potatoes, eggplant, cauliflower, and tomatoes, making it a natural addition to curries and vegetable dishes. Try also: using coriander in your own curry-powder blend; marinating vegetables with coriander and olive oil; tossing olives with toasted coriander seeds; mixing ground coriander into the batter for butter cakes and into sweet yeast breads.*

# BEEF CURRY

A long-simmering curry becomes a quick one when you substitute a tender cut of beef— sirloin—and stir-fry it till medium-rare. Serve the curry with steamed rice or potatoes.

 **WINE RECOMMENDATION** Either a shiraz from Australia or a syrah from California will provide enough flavor to stand up to this curry and contribute a black-pepper spiciness, too.

**SERVES 4**

3 tablespoons cooking oil

1 onion, cut into thin slices

3 cloves garlic, minced

1 tablespoon minced fresh ginger

2½ teaspoons ground coriander

1 teaspoon ground cumin

¼ teaspoon dried red-pepper flakes

⅛ teaspoon turmeric

½ teaspoon salt

2 tablespoons water

1½ pounds sirloin steak, cut into 1-inch cubes

3 tablespoons chopped cilantro

1. In a large frying pan, heat the oil over moderate heat. Add the onion and cook, stirring occasionally, until translucent, about 5 minutes. Add the garlic and ginger and cook, stirring, for 1 minute.

2. Meanwhile, in a small bowl, combine the coriander, cumin, red-pepper flakes, turmeric, salt, and water. Add the paste to the onion and cook, stirring, for 1 minute.

3. Add the meat to the pan and cook, stirring, for 3 minutes. Raise the heat to moderately high and cook to your taste, stirring, about 2 minutes longer for medium rare. Stir in the cilantro.

# PORK TENDERLOIN WITH PORT AND PRUNES

Coriander, which goes particularly well with pork, port, and prunes, gets a chance to shine with all three here. The spice coats the tenderloins as they roast and joins the wine and fruit in a sweet sauce for a subtle, interesting dish that couldn't be quicker or easier to prepare.

**WINE RECOMMENDATION**
A light-bodied or subtly flavored red wine would fade away next to the intense fruity flavors of this dish. Fortunately, lusty red zinfandels are widely available and will work perfectly.

**SERVES 4**

| | |
|---|---|
| 2 | pork tenderloins (about ¾ pound each) |
| 2½ | teaspoons ground coriander |
| ¾ | teaspoon salt |
| ¼ | teaspoon fresh-ground black pepper |
| 1½ | tablespoons cooking oil |
| ½ | cup port |
| ½ | cup canned low-sodium chicken broth or homemade stock |
| 20 | pitted prunes |
| 2 | tablespoons butter |

1. Heat the oven to 400°. Season the tenderloins with 2 teaspoons of the coriander, ½ teaspoon of the salt, and the pepper.

2. In a large ovenproof frying pan, heat the oil over moderately high heat. Add the tenderloins and brown on all sides, about 3 minutes. Put the pan in the oven and cook until the tenderloins are just done to medium, about 15 minutes.

Transfer the tenderloins to a carving board and leave to rest in a warm spot for about 5 minutes.

3. Pour off all the fat from the pan. Put the pan over moderate heat and add the port. Bring to a boil, scraping the bottom of the pan to dislodge any brown bits. Add the broth, prunes, and the remaining ¼ teaspoon salt. Boil until reduced to approximately ½ cup, about 3 minutes. Whisk in the remaining ½ teaspoon coriander and the butter. Slice the tenderloins and serve topped with the prunes and sauce.

**CUMIN** *If the dish is fiery, there's a good chance that cumin is one of the ingredients that contrast with the heat. In American chilies, Indian curries, and Mexican specialties, this aromatic spice stands up to blazing peppers, though its rich flavor improves many a milder dish, too. The most commonly available cumin seeds are light brown. The black variety has a stronger, more pungent flavor and is usually found only in Asian markets.* ✱ **USES** *Cumin grows well in warm climates, so it's not surprising that the spice is an integral part of the cuisines of India, North Africa, the Middle East, and Mexico. The savor of cumin is unmistakable in ready-made chili and curry powders. Its flavor pairs well with lamb, eggplant, and tomatoes, and it not only tastes good with dried beans and peas but may actually make them more digestible. Try also: sprinkling grilled lamb chops or kabobs with ground cumin and serving them with fresh tomato sauce; dusting chicken with cumin before broiling or roasting; stirring cumin and cream into cooked cabbage; adding it to refried beans; topping guacamole with a touch of toasted cumin; roasting winter squash flavored with cumin.*

# ROASTED CARROT AND CUMIN PUREE

Roasting carrots until they are golden brown brings out their sweetness and provides a perfect foil for tart lemon juice and musky cumin. Our silken puree is a particularly good side dish for lamb and also for roasted chicken.

**SERVES 4**

1½ pounds carrots (about 8 large), cut into ½-inch slices

2 tablespoons olive oil

1½ teaspoons ground cumin

Salt

¼ teaspoon fresh-ground black pepper

1 tablespoon butter

1 cup whole milk

½ teaspoon lemon juice

1. Heat the oven to 450°. In a roasting pan, combine the carrots with the oil, cumin, ¼ teaspoon salt, and the pepper. Roast the carrots, stirring occasionally, until tender and browned, about 20 minutes.

2. In a food processor, puree the carrots with the butter, milk, lemon juice, and ⅛ teaspoon salt. If necessary, reheat the puree in a small saucepan over low heat, stirring.

# CUMIN CHILI

You'll get a clear taste of cumin in this great cold-weather chili made with ground beef, beans, and green bell pepper. If you want a hotter chili, add as much cayenne as you like.

**WINE RECOMMENDATION**
Red zinfandel is just made for chili because it's as flavorful and fun as chili is. If you choose to make the dish spicy with cayenne, the ripe fruity character of zinfandel can even cool the heat.

**SERVES 4**

1½ tablespoons cooking oil

1 onion, chopped

1 green bell pepper, chopped

3 cloves garlic, minced

1½ pounds ground beef

3⅓ cups canned whole tomatoes with their juice (one 28-ounce can), broken up

2 tablespoons tomato paste

1 tablespoon ground cumin

1 teaspoon dried oregano

1 teaspoon salt

¼ teaspoon fresh-ground black pepper

1⅓ cups drained and rinsed canned pinto or kidney beans (one 15-ounce can)

1. In a large saucepan, heat the oil over moderately low heat. Add the onion, bell pepper, and garlic and cook, stirring, until the vegetables start to soften, about 10 minutes. Increase the heat to moderate. Add the ground beef and cook, stirring, until the meat is no longer pink, about 5 minutes.

2. Stir in the tomatoes, tomato paste, cumin, oregano, salt, and black pepper and bring to a simmer. Reduce the heat and simmer, partially covered, for 10 minutes. Add the beans and simmer, partially covered, until the vegetables are tender and the chili thickened, about 5 minutes longer.

---

## VARIATION

Add one ten-ounce package of frozen **corn**, thawed, to the chili along with the beans.

---

# LAMB MEATBALLS WITH CUMIN, MINT, AND TOMATO SAUCE

Mint, cumin, and chopped almonds give these delicious meatballs their Middle Eastern flavor. There's plenty of mint and cumin in the tomato sauce, too. Serve the meatballs and sauce over steamed couscous to be authentic. We think they're great over rice, too.

**WINE RECOMMENDATION**

Thanks to its warm cumin spiciness, refreshing herbal taste of mint, acidic tomatoes, and meaty lamb, this dish is a challenge to wine. A medium-bodied red that has crisp acidity, not too much tannin, and flavor that isn't too assertive is the best bet. Spain's famous Rioja is just such a wine; if possible, try an older one, indicated by the words *reserva* or *gran reserva* on the label.

**SERVES 4**

1½  pounds ground lamb

3  tablespoons chopped blanched almonds

3  tablespoons dried bread crumbs

5  tablespoons chopped fresh mint

2  cloves garlic, minced

2  teaspoons ground cumin

1½  teaspoons salt

¼  teaspoon fresh-ground black pepper

4  tablespoons cooking oil

1  onion, chopped

1⅔  cups crushed tomatoes in thick puree (from a 15-ounce can)

1. In a medium bowl, combine the lamb, almonds, bread crumbs, 3 tablespoons of the mint, the garlic, 1 teaspoon of the cumin, 1 teaspoon of the salt, and the pepper. Shape the mixture into 16 meatballs, about 2 inches in diameter.

2. In a large nonstick frying pan, heat 2 tablespoons of the oil over moderately high heat. Add the meatballs and cook, turning, until browned all over, about 3 minutes. Drain on paper towels.

3. In a large deep frying pan, heat the remaining 2 tablespoons oil over moderately low heat. Add the onion and cook, stirring occasionally, until translucent, about 5 minutes. Add the tomatoes and the remaining 1 teaspoon cumin and ½ teaspoon salt. Bring to a simmer, reduce the heat, and simmer, covered, for 10 minutes.

4. Add the meatballs to the tomato sauce and simmer, covered, until the meatballs are cooked through, about 10 minutes longer. Stir in the remaining 2 tablespoons mint.

**DILL SEEDS** The taste of dill seeds resembles that of caraway more than that of its own plant-mate, dill leaves. If the spice is not as well-known as the herb, it's because dill seeds are less commonly used on their own than as one of many pickling spices. These spices—a combination, in varying proportions, of dill seeds, peppercorns, yellow mustard seeds, dried red-pepper flakes, allspice berries, mace, cinnamon, and ginger—are essential to pickled fruits and vegetables, chutneys, and spiced vinegar. The seeds (or commercially the essential oils from the seeds) go into dill pickles, of course, along with the feathery leaves. Dill seeds are hard and, unless you want the crunch, require some cooking to soften them. ❀ **USES** Dill seeds are popular in Russia and Scandinavia in pickled dishes and creamy soups and sauces. Germans and Scandinavians sprinkle them in and on top of breads in the same way they do caraway seeds. Try also: stirring dill seeds into leek-and-potato soup or into sauerkraut; using the seeds to give extra flavor to creamed chicken, gratinéed potatoes, and braised celery or cucumber; adding dill seeds to whole-grain breads, breadsticks, or cheese straws.

# DILL-SEED BISCUITS

Dill seeds add a pleasant and unusual flavor to these flaky biscuits, which get their richness from both butter and heavy cream. Quick to make and to bake, the biscuits are best served warm with butter.

**MAKES 16 BISCUITS**

1¾  cups flour

4  teaspoons baking powder

2  teaspoons dill seeds

1  teaspoon salt

6  tablespoons cold unsalted butter, cut into
¼-inch pieces

1  cup heavy cream

1.  Heat the oven to 425°. In a medium bowl, whisk together the flour, baking powder, dill seeds, and salt. Cut or rub in the butter until the mixture is the texture of coarse meal with a few pea-size pieces remaining. Stir in the cream with a fork just until the dough comes together.

2.  On a lightly floured surface, knead the dough gently just until smooth, about 5 times. Roll the dough ¾ inch thick. Using a 2-inch round cutter, stamp out circles of the dough. Put them, about ½ inch apart, on an ungreased baking sheet. Roll out the scraps in the same way. Stamp out more circles and put them on the baking sheet.

3.  Bake the biscuits in the middle of the oven until golden brown, 12 to 15 minutes.

# CORN AND SHRIMP CHOWDER WITH MASHED POTATOES

Simmering dill seeds with corn and shrimp makes a delectable soup. Instead of the traditional cubes of potato throughout the chowder, we've put a mound of creamy mashed potatoes in the center of the bowl. This comforting dish is a meal in itself.

**WINE RECOMMENDATION**
The slight sweetness of the corn and the richness of the cream or milk require a flavorful white wine, but avoid oaky ones, which can clash with the shrimp. A New York, Oregon, or German riesling would work well.

**SERVES 4**

| | |
|---|---|
| 1 | tablespoon cooking oil |
| 1 | onion, chopped |
| 1 | carrot, chopped |
| 1 | clove garlic, chopped |
| 3½ | cups canned low-sodium chicken broth or homemade stock |
| 1 | teaspoon dill seeds |
| 2 | pounds red new potatoes (about 12), cut in half, or boiling potatoes (about 6), cut into quarters |
| 2 | teaspoons salt |
| | Fresh-ground black pepper |
| 6 | tablespoons butter, at room temperature |
| 1 | cup light cream or milk |
| 3 | cups fresh (cut from about 5 ears) or frozen corn kernels |
| 1½ | pounds medium shrimp, shelled |
| 2 | tablespoons chopped fresh parsley |

1. In a large saucepan, heat the oil over moderately low heat. Add the onion, carrot, and garlic and cook, stirring occasionally, until the onion is translucent, about 5 minutes. Add the broth and dill seeds and bring to a boil. Reduce the heat and simmer, covered, for about 20 minutes.

2. Meanwhile, put the potatoes in a medium saucepan of salted water. Bring to a boil, reduce the heat, and simmer until tender, about 15 minutes. Drain the potatoes and put them back into the saucepan along with ¾ teaspoon of the salt and a pinch of pepper. Mash the potatoes over very low heat, gradually incorporating the butter and ¾ cup of the cream. Keep warm.

3. Add the corn and ½ teaspoon of the salt to the broth and simmer, covered, until the corn is just tender, about 15 minutes. In a food processor or blender, puree the chowder and then pour it back into the saucepan. Add the shrimp and the remaining ¾ teaspoon salt. Bring to a simmer and cook until the shrimp are almost done, about 1 minute. Stir in the remaining ¼ cup cream, the parsley, and ⅛ teaspoon pepper and bring just back to a simmer. Reheat the potatoes, if necessary. Spoon them into the center of four bowls and pour the chowder around them.

**FENNEL SEEDS** *Though they come from two different plants, fennel seeds and aniseeds are similar in appearance and taste and can often be used almost interchangeably. Fennel seeds come from the familiar plant native to southern Europe, which is grown primarily for its bulbous stalk. The type most commonly available is Florence fennel, the seeds of which have a mild anise flavor. Aniseeds, which come from another member of the parsley family, are native to the Middle East and are stronger than fennel seeds.* ❁ **USES** *Fennel seeds are important in Italian and Greek cooking and also in Chinese, Indian, and Egyptian foods. Whereas anise is a popular flavoring for drinks—ouzo in Greece, anís in Spain, and pastis in France—its cousin fennel seed is more likely to be found in savory dishes like sausages, meat sauces for pasta, curries, breads, and crackers. Fennel and aniseeds sometimes make a joint appearance in the famous French fish soup bouillabaisse. Try also: stirring fennel seeds into tomato sauce, braised cabbage, or veal stew; adding aniseeds to cakes and cookies, especially those that contain fruit or nuts.*

# CHOCOLATE FENNEL PUDDING

A hint of fennel is an unexpected and delicious addition to classic chocolate pudding. If you like, serve the pudding topped with lightly sweetened whipped cream. You can use aniseeds in place of the fennel seeds; the flavor will be more pronounced.

**SERVES 4**

2 cups milk

1 cup heavy cream

2 tablespoons unsweetened cocoa powder

2½ tablespoons fennel seeds, chopped

4 large egg yolks

⅓ cup sugar

3 tablespoons cornstarch

Pinch salt

2 ounces bittersweet chocolate, chopped

1. In a medium stainless-steel saucepan, bring the milk, ⅔ cup of the cream, the cocoa, and the fennel seeds to a boil, whisking occasionally. Remove from the heat and let the mixture infuse, covered, for 10 minutes.

2. In a medium bowl, whisk the egg yolks, sugar, cornstarch, and salt until pale yellow.

3. Bring the milk mixture back to a boil and then strain it into the egg mixture. Whisk until smooth and pour back into the saucepan. Cook over moderately high heat, whisking constantly, until the mixture comes to a boil, about 1 minute. Remove from the heat.

4. Add the chocolate and whisk until melted. Whisk in the remaining ⅓ cup cream. Pour the pudding into individual bowls and chill.

# BAKED SAUSAGES, FENNEL, AND POTATOES WITH FONTINA

Fennel seeds in the tomato sauce boost the flavor of the sliced fennel bulb in this satisfying dish. A thin layer of fontina cheese on top bakes to a golden brown. For a spicy version, use hot Italian sausages rather than mild.

**WINE RECOMMENDATION**

More often than not, red wine is best with sausage, but the relative delicacy of this delicious dish will shine through better with a crisp, herbal-flavored white wine, such as an inexpensive white Bordeaux from France.

**SERVES 4**

- 2 tablespoons cooking oil
- 1 pound mild Italian sausages
- 1 onion, cut into thin slices
- 1 fennel bulb, cored and cut into thin slices
- 2 cloves garlic, minced
- ¾ teaspoon fennel seeds
- 1 pound baking potatoes (about 2), peeled and cut into ¾-inch cubes
- ½ teaspoon salt
- ⅓ cup dry white wine
- 3½ cups canned tomatoes (one 28-ounce can), drained and chopped
- 6 ounces fontina, grated (about 1½ cups)

1. Heat the oven to 450°. In a large deep frying pan, heat 1 tablespoon of the oil over moderate heat. Add the sausages and cook until browned and cooked through, about 10 minutes. Remove.

When the sausages are cool enough to handle, cut them into ¼-inch slices.

2. Add the remaining 1 tablespoon oil to the pan and heat over moderately low heat. Add the onion, fennel bulb, garlic, and fennel seeds and cook, covered, for 5 minutes. Stir in the potatoes and salt and cook, covered, until the vegetables start to soften, about 5 minutes.

3. Stir in the wine and simmer until evaporated. Stir in the tomatoes. Raise the heat to moderately high and simmer until no liquid remains in the pan, 2 to 3 minutes longer. Stir in the sausages and transfer the mixture to a 9-by-13-inch baking dish.

4. Bake the sausage mixture for 10 minutes. Remove from the oven and top with the fontina. Bake until the vegetables are tender and the cheese is melted, about 10 minutes longer.

**GINGER** *The same rhizome of the ginger plant that heats up Asian stir-fries and Indian curries is dried and pulverized to make the common, and still slightly hot, ground ginger used in gingerbread, ginger puddings, gingersnaps, and ginger ale. Ground ginger is most often found linked with sugar. Since the flavor of ground ginger is less immediate and intense than that of fresh, dried can't be considered a good substitute for gingerroot, but in a pinch, powdered ginger is better than none at all, even in savory dishes.* ❊ **USES** *In addition to its role in baked goods, ground ginger is present in three important spice blends: pickling spice used to pickle vegetables, mixed spice or pudding spice used in England in steamed puddings, and quatre-épices, a French blend used in charcuterie and long-simmered meat dishes. Try also: adding ground ginger to pot roast; sprinkling ground ginger on acorn or butternut squash before baking; adding it to cranberry sauce; sprinkling it on melon or peaches; spicing up shortbread with ground ginger; using it in lemon and chocolate cakes and cookies; stirring it into apple-pancake batter.*

# GINGER-SPICED PECANS

Pecan halves sautéed with butter, sugar, and ground ginger are positively addictive. Serve them with ice cream, a selection of cookies, or fruit desserts, or on their own after dessert as petits fours. They're quick to make and, presented in tins, are great holiday gifts. If you prepare the pecans more than two days ahead, add another half teaspoon of ginger, since the flavor dissipates over time.

**MAKES 3 CUPS**

4 tablespoons unsalted butter

3 cups pecan halves

¼ cup sugar

2 teaspoons ground ginger

Pinch salt

1. In a large nonstick frying pan, melt the butter over moderate heat. Add the pecans and cook, stirring, until beginning to brown, about 4 minutes.

2. In a small bowl, combine the sugar, ginger, and salt. Sprinkle the mixture evenly over the pecans in the pan and cook, stirring, until the pecans are coated with the sugar mixture and are browned and crisp, 1 to 2 minutes. Don't cook them too long or the sugar will begin to melt.

3. Put the pecans on a baking sheet and spread them out to cool.

# INDIAN PUDDING

With its delightful contrasts of warm spicy pudding and cold vanilla ice cream, this version of an American classic is the ultimate comfort dessert. Homey as it is, though, it looks elegant when served in stemmed bowls. While Indian pudding is frequently stodgy, our version is soft and light and altogether tempting.

**SERVES 4**

    2   cups whole milk
    1   cup heavy cream
    ½   cup molasses
    ¼   cup dark brown sugar
    ⅓   cup cornmeal
    1   teaspoon ground ginger
    1   teaspoon cinnamon
    ¼   teaspoon salt
    1   pint vanilla ice cream

1.  Heat the oven to 350°. In a medium heavy stainless-steel saucepan, bring the milk, cream, molasses, and brown sugar almost to a simmer over moderately high heat, stirring occasionally.

2.  In a medium bowl, whisk together the cornmeal, ginger, cinnamon, and salt. Add to the milk mixture, whisking. Bring just to a simmer, whisking. Pour into an 8-by-8-inch baking dish. The batter will be thin and shallow.

3.  Bake the pudding in the middle of the oven for 20 minutes. Remove from the oven and stir well. Return the pudding to the oven and continue cooking for 20 minutes. The pudding will still be quite wobbly but will set as it cools. Let cool on a rack for 20 minutes and serve warm. Or cool completely and reheat the pudding in a 350° oven for about 5 minutes just before serving. Serve the pudding topped with the ice cream.

## VARIATIONS

Stir the pudding after it has baked for twenty minutes and then top it with one-third cup of chopped **pecans** or **walnuts**. Continue baking as directed for twenty minutes longer.

*Strong enough to stand up to the gamiest game and the sourest sauerkraut, juniper berries are surprisingly sweet and have a pleasantly resinous taste that befits their source, an evergreen shrub. The bluish-black berries, which vary in potency depending on where they were grown and when they were picked, can be left whole for pickles or broths, crushed to release their flavor during cooking, or ground to a fine powder in a spice grinder.* ❁ **USES** *Juniper is the major flavoring in gin. It complements wild game, especially venison and boar, and is also excellent with pork, lamb, chestnuts, cabbage, and apples. It can season marinades, beef stews, and, often, pâtés. Try also: braising chicken with diced ham, mushrooms, and a few crushed juniper berries; stuffing the cavity of a Cornish hen with juniper berries and sprigs of rosemary; making a quick pan sauce for pork chops with cream and juniper berries; sautéing a ham steak, throwing in some juniper berries and raisins, and deglazing the pan with cider; adding the berries to warm cider or including them in applesauce.*

# POTATO GRATIN WITH JUNIPER BERRIES

Juniper berries add intrigue to potatoes baked with broth and topped with crisp golden bread crumbs. Serve this gratin with virtually any simply cooked meat or poultry.

**SERVES 4**

3 tablespoons butter

1 cup canned low-sodium chicken broth or homemade stock

8 juniper berries

2 pounds baking potatoes, peeled and cut crosswise into ⅛-inch-thick slices

1 clove garlic, minced

1 teaspoon salt

¼ teaspoon fresh-ground black pepper

1½ cups fresh bread crumbs

1. Heat the oven to 425°. Butter an 8-by-12-inch baking dish with ½ tablespoon of the butter. In a blender, puree ¼ cup of the stock with the juniper berries. Put the mixture in a small saucepan with the remaining ¾ cup stock; bring to a simmer.

2. Layer half of the potatoes in the dish and top with the garlic, ½ teaspoon of the salt, and ⅛ teaspoon of the pepper. Dot with ½ tablespoon of the butter. Add the remaining potatoes to the dish and sprinkle with the remaining ½ teaspoon salt and ⅛ teaspoon pepper. Pour the simmering broth over the potatoes. Dot with 1 tablespoon of the butter and cover the dish with aluminum foil. Bake the potatoes for 20 minutes. Remove the aluminum foil and bake 10 minutes longer.

3. Meanwhile, in a small saucepan, melt the remaining 1 tablespoon butter and stir in the bread crumbs. Sprinkle them on the potatoes and continue baking until the potatoes are tender and the bread crumbs are golden, about 15 minutes longer.

# BRAISED CHICKEN THIGHS WITH SAUERKRAUT

Sauerkraut simmered with vegetables, apple, and juniper berries is a perfect match for bacon and chicken thighs. The robust combination of flavors makes this a great hearty winter dish.

**WINE RECOMMENDATION**
For a white wine that will contrast nicely with the sauerkraut, look for a soft, full-flavored, and unoaked white. Gewürztraminer or pinot gris from Alsace in France are ideal choices.

**SERVES 4**

- 3 slices bacon, cut crosswise into thin strips
- 8 chicken thighs (about 2½ pounds in all)
- ¾ teaspoon salt
- ¼ teaspoon fresh-ground black pepper
- 1 onion, chopped
- 1 carrot, chopped
- 1 tart apple, such as Granny Smith, peeled, cored, and chopped
- 3 cups drained and rinsed sauerkraut (about 1½ pounds)
- 1 cup canned low-sodium chicken broth or homemade stock
- 1 teaspoon Dijon mustard
- 10 juniper berries, lightly crushed
- 1 bay leaf

1. In a large deep frying pan, cook the bacon over moderate heat until crisp. Remove with a slotted spoon and reserve.

2. Season the chicken thighs with ½ teaspoon of the salt and the pepper and add to the pan in batches if necessary. Cook, turning, until browned, about 8 minutes. Remove from the pan. Pour off all but 1 tablespoon of the fat.

3. Add the onion, carrot, and apple to the pan. Cook over moderate heat, covered, for 5 minutes. Stir in the sauerkraut, bacon, broth, the remaining ¼ teaspoon salt, the mustard, juniper berries, and bay leaf. Arrange the chicken in an even layer on top. Bring to a simmer, reduce the heat, and cook, covered, until the chicken is just done, about 25 minutes.

4. Remove the chicken from the pan and discard the bay leaf. If too much liquid remains in the pan, raise the heat to moderately high and cook until slightly thickened. Serve the sauerkraut topped with the chicken.

## MUSTARD SEEDS

*Bite into a single mustard seed, and it fills your whole mouth with heat. The most common mustard seeds—the yellow ones—are also the mildest, relatively speaking. Next come the hot and bitter brown seeds and finally the particularly powerful black seeds, available in Indian shops. Mustard seeds are ground into powdered dry mustard; ground and mixed with vinegar, salt, and spices to make prepared mustard; and also sold whole. To bring out the sharp flavor of powdered mustard, mix it with a small amount of cool liquid; after about ten minutes, an enzymatic reaction occurs, giving the spice its telltale pungency. To boost the taste of whole mustard seeds, toast them in a dry frying pan, or sauté them in a little oil until they pop, which brings out a flood of flavor.* ❀ **USES** *Mustard seeds are often used for pickling, while powdered mustard dissolved in a bit of water is an English classic with roast beef. Try also: making a nice crust of mustard seeds atop roasted salmon; adding them to the oil before sautéing broccoli or Brussels sprouts; enhancing Welsh rarebit with dry mustard; stirring it into sour cream for a sauce to serve with cold ham, beef, or poached fish.*

# SMOKED PORK CHOPS STUFFED WITH GRUYÈRE AND MUSTARD

Tender, delicious smoked pork chops are already cooked by the smoking process and so need only to be heated through before serving. The stuffing here features both whole mustard seeds and prepared mustard.

**WINE RECOMMENDATION**
A crisp, dry, but full-bodied white, such as a Mâcon-Villages, from the Burgundy region of France, will be terrific with these chops.

**SERVES 4**

| | |
|---|---|
| 1 | tablespoon yellow mustard seeds |
| 1½ | tablespoons Dijon mustard |
| 4 | smoked pork chops (about 1¾ pounds in all) |
| 2 | ounces Gruyère, cut into 4 thin slices |
| ⅛ | teaspoon fresh-ground black pepper |

1. Heat the oven to 425°. In a small bowl, combine the mustard seeds and Dijon mustard. Cut a pocket, horizontally, in the side of each chop. Spread the inside of the pockets with the mustard mixture and stuff each with a slice of the cheese. Close each pocket with a toothpick or small skewer.

2. Put the chops in a baking dish and sprinkle them with the pepper. Bake the chops until the cheese melts, about 15 minutes. Remove toothpicks or skewers before serving.

# Sautéed Catfish with Mustard Sauce

Dry mustard can be intensely hot, much more so than most prepared mustards. We've used it to make a creamy sauce and paired it with crisp cornmeal-coated catfish.

**WINE RECOMMENDATION**
German rieslings are tremendously flexible with food. A classic riesling, one that is not fully dry, is ideal for cooling the heat of the mustard and cutting through the rich cream, too.

**SERVES 4**

¾  cup plus 1 tablespoon heavy cream

4  teaspoons dry mustard

1  egg, beaten to mix

1  cup cornmeal

1¼  teaspoons salt

½  teaspoon fresh-ground black pepper

1½  pounds catfish fillets

3  tablespoons cooking oil

½  cup canned low-sodium chicken broth or homemade stock

1  clove garlic, minced

1. In a small bowl, combine ¼ cup of the cream and the mustard. Let sit about 10 minutes.

2. In a shallow dish, combine the egg with the 1 tablespoon cream. In another shallow dish, combine the cornmeal with 1 teaspoon of the salt and the pepper. Dip the fillets into the egg mixture and then into the seasoned cornmeal. Shake off the excess cornmeal.

3. In a large nonstick frying pan, heat 2 tablespoons of the oil over moderate heat. Add half the cornmeal-coated fish and fry, turning once, until the fillets are golden on the outside and just done in the center, about 4 minutes per side for ¾-inch-thick fillets. Drain the fish on paper towels. Repeat with the remaining 1 tablespoon oil and fish fillets. Wipe out the pan.

4. Put the pan over moderate heat. Add the broth and garlic and bring to a simmer. Stir in the remaining ½ cup cream; simmer until reduced to approximately ⅓ cup, about 2 minutes. Stir in the reserved mustard cream and the remaining ¼ teaspoon salt and simmer until warm through, about 1 minute longer. Serve the catfish fillets topped with the sauce.

NUTMEG *Grating beautifully grained and speckled whole nutmeg is a visual as well as an aromatic pleasure and is as easy as spooning the already grated stuff out of a jar. Just-grated nutmeg tastes and smells much more intense than the packaged variety. Little nutmeg graters are available in cookware stores for this purpose, but any small grater will do. Not only is the inside of a nutmeg pretty, but the nutmeg shell has a lacy, brilliant-orange coating (which is dried to make mace, a similar but milder spice), and surrounding that is a yellow plum, of which the nutmeg forms the pit.*
❋ **USES** *Long a favorite in cakes, cookies, puddings, custards, and pies, nutmeg is also traditional in hot and cold drinks, such as eggnog, hot wine, punch, and posset. In India, nutmeg goes into meat dishes; the English use it in their traditional bread sauce; Italians put it in cheese-filled pasta; and the French use it in pâtés and sausages, with spinach, and in cream sauces. Try also: sprinkling nutmeg on cheese soup, cheesecake, or French toast; tossing fettuccine with sautéed mushrooms, cream, Parmesan, and nutmeg; adding it to poached fruit; stirring it into softened vanilla ice cream and then refreezing.*

# NUTMEG SHORTBREAD

Nutmeg makes a scintillating addition to rich, buttery shortbread. Though these cookies bake for about fifty minutes, the actual work time is amazingly brief for something so special. If you cook the shortbread in a black pan, check it after forty minutes since the color of the pan will cause the dough to cook more quickly. Shortbread keeps well stored in tins.

**MAKES 8 TRIANGLES**

1⅓ cups flour

1 teaspoon grated nutmeg

¼ pound cold unsalted butter, cut into ¼-inch cubes

6 tablespoons sugar

1 large egg yolk

1. Heat the oven to 325°. Butter an 8-inch round metal cake or pie pan.

2. In a medium bowl, whisk together the flour and ¾ teaspoon of the nutmeg. With your fingers, rub in the butter completely until the mixture is the texture of sand. Using a fork, stir in 5 tablespoons of the sugar. Stir in the egg yolk. Press the mixture together to make a dry, crumbly dough and put it on a work surface. Knead the dough about twelve times until it just holds together.

3. Press the dough in an even layer into the prepared pan. With a small, sharp knife, mark eight wedges halfway into the dough. With a fork, prick the dough every ½ inch or so. In a small bowl, combine the remaining 1 tablespoon sugar and ¼ teaspoon nutmeg and sprinkle it on the dough. Bake the shortbread in the middle of the oven until golden, 50 to 55 minutes.

4. Let the shortbread cool slightly in the pan set on a rack and then cut into wedges. Let cool completely in the pan.

# BAKED RIGATONI WITH SPINACH, RICOTTA, AND FONTINA

A quick take on spinach and ricotta cannelloni, this baked pasta is fast because there's nothing to stuff. The filling is simply tossed with cooked rigatoni that's then topped with fontina and baked to a golden brown.

### ■ WINE RECOMMENDATION

A delicately flavored white such as Orvieto will complement the mild ricotta nicely. And, because Orvieto is not oaky, the wine has no bitter tannin to clash with the slightly bitter spinach and nutmeg.

### SERVES 4

- 1 pound rigatoni
- 3 tablespoons olive oil
- 1 10-ounce package frozen spinach, thawed
- 2 cups (about 1 pound) ricotta
- 5 tablespoons grated Parmesan
- ½ teaspoon grated nutmeg
- ¾ teaspoon salt
- ¼ teaspoon fresh-ground black pepper
- 6 ounces fontina, grated (about 1½ cups)

1. Heat the oven to 450°. Oil a 9-by-13-inch baking dish.

2. In a large pot of boiling, salted water, cook the rigatoni until almost done, about 12 minutes. Drain. Put the pasta in the prepared baking dish and toss with 1 tablespoon of the oil.

3. Meanwhile, squeeze as much of the water as possible from the spinach. Put the spinach in a food processor and puree with the ricotta, 3 tablespoons of the Parmesan, the nutmeg, salt, and pepper. Stir in half the fontina.

4. Stir the spinach mixture into the pasta. Top with the remaining fontina and Parmesan. Drizzle the remaining 2 tablespoons oil over the top. Bake the pasta until the top is golden brown, 15 to 20 minutes.

---

## VARIATION

You can substitute another chunky pasta, such as **penne rigate**, **penne**, **ziti**, or **fusilli**. Boil all of these one or two minutes less.

---

 *Check the label when you're purchasing paprika. This ground red pepper can be mild or it can be surprisingly hot, but it always gives fair warning: If it's hot, it will be marked as such on the label. Paprika shares both its color and its considerable flavor with any food it touches. Though the spice originated in Mexico and is now produced in Spain, the United States, and other countries, it's in Hungary that paprika found its culinary home. Hungarian paprika is generally considered to be the highest quality. Look for a bright-red color; as the spice ages and loses flavor, it turns reddish brown.* ❋ **USES** *Paprika is prevalent in the cuisines of Spain (something made Galician style is sure to include the spice) and Morocco, as well as that of Mexico. Hungary, of course, is famous for its goulash and veal paprikás. Try also: stirring paprika into fried potatoes and onions; flavoring rice with paprika; mixing some of the spice into lentil soup with sausages; adding hot paprika to macaroni and cheese; sautéing shrimp in olive oil with garlic and paprika; steaming clams in paprika-spiked tomato broth; tossing cubes of swordfish with oil, lemon juice, and paprika before grilling them on skewers.*

# CHICKEN BREASTS WITH CHARMOULA

Charmoula, the intense Moroccan spice sauce, tastes wonderful with fish as well as chicken. Keep an eye on the spices as they toast in the dry pan so that they don't burn.

 **WINE RECOMMENDATION**
A white with a bit of sweetness, like an Oregon pinot gris, will play off the spicy sauce nicely.

**SERVES 4**

- 1 tablespoon plus ¼ teaspoon paprika
- 1 teaspoon ground cumin
- 2 cloves garlic, smashed
- ⅓ cup lightly packed cilantro leaves, plus 8 sprigs (optional) for garnish
- ⅓ cup lightly packed flat-leaf parsley leaves
- 7 tablespoons olive oil
  Grated zest of half an orange
- 2 tablespoons lemon juice
- ¼ teaspoon cayenne
- ¾ teaspoon salt
  Fresh-ground black pepper

- 4 boneless, skinless chicken breasts (about 1⅓ pounds in all)
- 2 plum tomatoes, diced (optional)

1. In a small frying pan, toast the 1 tablespoon paprika with the cumin over low heat, stirring, until fragrant, about 30 seconds. Put in a blender and puree with the garlic, cilantro leaves, parsley, 6 tablespoons of the oil, the orange zest, lemon juice, cayenne, ½ teaspoon of the salt, and ¼ teaspoon black pepper. Leave in the blender.

2. Put 1 tablespoon oil in a nonstick frying pan over moderate heat. Season the chicken with ¼ teaspoon salt, ¼ teaspoon paprika, and ⅛ teaspoon black pepper. Brown 5 minutes. Turn; cook until just done, 4 to 5 minutes longer. Blend the sauce to re-emulsify; serve over the chicken. Sprinkle with the tomatoes and top with the cilantro sprigs.

# SAUSAGE AND POTATO QUESADILLAS

These substantial double-decker quesadillas call for fresh (not the more common dried) chorizo sausage, which is generally made with paprika. If you can't find fresh chorizo, use another sausage, such as hot Italian, in its place. Or use a mild sausage and add an extra half teaspoon of hot paprika.

**WINE RECOMMENDATION**

Many Portuguese reds have rustic personalities that will suit the mood of this dish well. The rich, hefty wines from the Dão or Douro regions are your best bets, but even the medium-bodied reds from elsewhere in Portugal have enough substance to stand up to chorizo.

**SERVES 4**

1 pound fresh chorizo or other sausages, casings removed

1 tablespoon plus 1 teaspoon cooking oil

1 baking potato (about ½ pound), peeled and cut into ¼-inch cubes

¾ teaspoon hot paprika

¼ teaspoon salt

12 6-inch flour tortillas

¼ cup chopped red onion

½ cup cilantro leaves

½ pound Monterey jack, grated (about 2 cups)

1. Heat the oven to 425°. In a large nonstick frying pan, cook the sausage over moderately high heat, breaking it up with a fork, until browned, about 5 minutes. With a slotted spoon, remove the sausage from the pan. Pour off the fat from the pan.

2. Heat the 1 tablespoon oil in the pan over moderate heat. Add the potato, ½ teaspoon of the paprika, and the salt and cook, stirring occasionally, until tender, about 10 minutes.

3. Put four of the tortillas on a work surface. Put half of the sausage, potato, onion, cilantro, and cheese on the tortillas, spreading the ingredients all the way to the edge, and top with four more tortillas. Repeat with the remaining sausage, potato, onion, cilantro, and cheese and cover with the remaining four tortillas.

4. Brush the tops of the quesadillas with the remaining 1 teaspoon oil and sprinkle with the remaining ¼ teaspoon paprika. Put the quesadillas on a baking sheet and bake until the cheese melts, about 5 minutes. Cut into wedges and serve.

**PEPPER** *The most ubiquitous of spices, pepper accounts for one quarter of the world's spice trade. This global favorite starts out as small green berries growing on vines in India, Indonesia, Malaysia, or Brazil. The unripe berries can be dried or pickled as green peppercorns, fermented and dried to make black peppercorns, or left on the vines to ripen to red, then skinned and dried into the less flavorful white peppercorns. Two other types—pink and Szechuan—are berries from entirely different plants, not related to common black pepper at all. Whole peppercorns last indefinitely, but the flavor vanishes quickly once they're ground. Grind black pepper from a mill (the result is far superior to preground pepper) and add it just before serving. For long-simmered recipes, whole peppercorns are best.* ❀ **USES** *Pepper is prized around the world for its lively heat. It accentuates the taste of almost everything, whether meat, vegetable, or even fruit—especially pears, figs, and strawberries. Try also: making thin, crisp biscuits with pepper to serve with cocktails; flavoring corn on the cob with pepper as well as salt; grinding black pepper over sautéed pears drizzled with honey and a touch of balsamic vinegar.*

# BERRY FOOL WITH BLACK PEPPER

Black pepper is an unlikely and stimulating addition to this dessert of fresh strawberries in whipped cream flavored with raspberry puree and Grand Marnier.

**SERVES 4**

1⅓ cups fresh raspberries (6 ounces), or the same quantity of frozen raspberries, thawed

½ cup sugar

1 teaspoon fresh-ground black pepper

3 tablespoons Grand Marnier or other orange liqueur

1½ cups heavy cream

1 quart strawberries (1 pound), 4 reserved, the rest hulled and halved

1. In a small saucepan, combine the raspberries and sugar. Cook over low heat, covered, stirring occasionally, until the berries are soft and the sugar dissolved, 5 to 10 minutes. Strain into a medium bowl, pressing the berries to get all the juice. Stir in the pepper. Chill until completely cold, about 20 minutes. Stir in the Grand Marnier.

2. In a large bowl, beat the cream just until it holds firm peaks when the beaters are lifted. Fold in the raspberry mixture and the halved strawberries until just combined. Serve in stemmed glasses or bowls, topped with the reserved whole strawberries.

# SPAGHETTI WITH SHIITAKES, PARMESAN, AND PEPPER

Here's a great weeknight pasta that highlights one of our favorite mushrooms and takes only minutes to prepare. The combination of earthy shiitakes and sharp cheese is perfect with lots of black pepper.

**WINE RECOMMENDATION**
The mix of flavors opens the door to all sorts of wine choices. To match the earthiness of the mushrooms, try a white based on the chardonnay grape; a Bourgogne Blanc from France would be particularly good. To echo the black pepper, look for a red with a similar flavor, such as a dolcetto from Italy or a petite sirah from California.

**SERVES 4**

4 tablespoons olive oil

1 pound shiitake mushrooms, stems removed, caps cut into thin slices

¾ teaspoon fresh-ground black pepper

¼ teaspoon salt

2 cloves garlic, minced

1½ cups canned low-sodium chicken broth or homemade stock

¾ pound spaghetti

½ cup grated Parmesan, plus more for serving

1. In a large frying pan, heat 2 tablespoons of the oil over moderate heat. Add the mushrooms, ½ teaspoon of the pepper, and the salt and cook, stirring occasionally, until the mushrooms are browned, 5 to 10 minutes.

2. Add the garlic and cook, stirring, for 30 seconds. Add the broth and bring to a simmer. Cook until reduced to about 1 cup, 2 to 3 minutes.

3. Meanwhile, in a large pot of boiling, salted water, cook the spaghetti until just done, about 12 minutes. Drain. Toss the spaghetti with the mushroom sauce, the remaining 2 tablespoons oil and ¼ teaspoon pepper, and the Parmesan. Serve with more cheese.

## VARIATION

Add a couple of tablespoons chopped fresh herbs, such as **chives**, **tarragon**, **thyme**, or **parsley**, to the spaghetti along with the Parmesan.

## RED PEPPER

*For the cook in search of spiciness, there's no more versatile supplier of fire than dried red chile peppers. You can buy them whole, crushed into dried red-pepper flakes, or finely ground into cayenne or pure chile powder (not the spice mix called chili powder). Chile powder varies in the strength of its heat according to the variety of pepper, but cayenne is always hot.* ❈ **USES** *Many cuisines have a favorite hot sauce based on some form of red pepper. Americans have Tabasco sauce; Jamaicans, not content with only one, produce several liquid hot sauces; Tunisians enjoy harissa; and Indonesian sambal paste ignites curries and rice. Cayenne's affinity for shellfish, especially crab, shrimp, and oysters, makes it the ideal spice for such Acadian dishes as jambalaya and gumbo. Try also: adding red-pepper flakes to tomato or garlic-and-oil sauces for pasta; perking up sautéed broccoli or braised Swiss chard with pepper flakes; using whole or flaked peppers in Asian noodle dishes, Szechuan stir-fries, and Thai satays; putting just a pinch or two of cayenne in rich sauces like mayonnaise, hollandaise, and béchamel.*

# CANADIAN BACON AND MOZZARELLA PENNE

Hot red-pepper flakes offer a pleasant contrast to mild mozzarella and salty Canadian bacon. To turn this into a satisfying vegetarian pasta, just leave out the bacon.

**WINE RECOMMENDATION**
A crisp red based on the barbera grape will be heavenly with this spicy, tomatoey sauce.

**SERVES 4**

½ pound fresh mozzarella, cut into ½-inch cubes

1 clove garlic, minced

2½ tablespoons olive oil

¾ teaspoon salt

Dried red-pepper flakes

¼ cup chopped fresh parsley

1 small onion, chopped

1½ cups canned crushed tomatoes in thick puree (one 15-ounce can)

¼ cup water

¾ pound penne

½ pound Canadian bacon, cut into ¼-inch dice

1. In a small bowl, combine the mozzarella, garlic, 1½ tablespoons of the oil, ¼ teaspoon of the salt, ¼ teaspoon red-pepper flakes, and the parsley.

2. In a large saucepan, heat the remaining 1 tablespoon oil over moderately low heat. Cook the onion, stirring occasionally, until translucent, about 5 minutes. Add the tomatoes, water, the remaining ½ teaspoon salt, and a pinch of red-pepper flakes. Reduce the heat and simmer, covered, for 15 minutes.

3. In a large pot of boiling, salted water, cook the pasta until just done, about 13 minutes. Reserve ¼ cup of the pasta-cooking water. Drain. Toss the pasta with the tomato sauce, mozzarella mixture, and Canadian bacon. If the sauce seems too thick, add some of the reserved pasta-cooking water.

# CHICKEN AND SAUSAGE JAMBALAYA

Between the *andouille* sausage and the cayenne, this is one spicy dish. With plenty of rice, vegetables, and chicken in the pot, it's also a satisfying dinner. If you can't find *andouille* and need to substitute a milder sausage, increase the cayenne to one-half teaspoon.

**WINE RECOMMENDATION**

The somewhat vegetal flavors of the sauvignon blanc grape will be right at home here. Try one from the United States (sometimes called *Fumé Blanc*). It will have enough richness to stand up to the sausage.

**SERVES 4**

1   tablespoon cooking oil

½   pound *andouille* or hot link sausages

1   large onion, chopped

2   ribs celery, chopped

1   green bell pepper, chopped

2   cloves garlic, minced

1½   cups long-grain rice

3   cups canned low-sodium chicken broth or homemade stock

¼   teaspoon cayenne

2   bay leaves

1½   teaspoons salt

1   pound boneless, skinless chicken breasts (about 3 in all), cut into 1-inch pieces

1. In a large saucepan, heat the oil over moderate heat. Add the sausages and cook, turning, until browned, 5 to 10 minutes in all. Remove. When the sausages are cool enough to handle, cut them into ¼-inch slices. Pour off all but 1 tablespoon fat from the pan.

2. Add the onion, celery, bell pepper, and garlic to the pan and cook, covered, over moderately low heat until the vegetables start to soften, about 5 minutes. Add the rice, broth, sausage, cayenne, bay leaves, and salt and bring to a boil. Reduce the heat and simmer, covered, for 15 minutes.

3. Stir in the chicken and simmer, covered, until the chicken is just done and the rice and the vegetables are tender, about 5 minutes longer. Remove from the heat and let stand, covered, for about 2 minutes.

**SAFFRON** *Delicate, golden threads of saffron are expensive to buy, and well they should be. They're the dried stigmas of crocus flowers, and each one is collected by hand, one at a time. It takes about a hundred thousand of them to equal a pound, but it takes only a pinch to endow food with saffron's distinctive flavor and its fantastic reddish-yellow hue. If possible, choose saffron threads rather than powder, which can be adulterated and undoubtedly has been if the saffron comes cheap. Either crush the threads with your fingertips directly into the cooking food or infuse the threads into liquid before adding them to the dish. Most of the saffron available is already dried, but if you're using Indian saffron, toast the threads in a frying pan (without oil) before crushing them.* ❀ **USES** *Many of the world's classic dishes depend on saffron for their character: French bouillabaisse, Spanish paella, Italian risotto Milanese. It's often present in Moroccan stews and couscous and, of course, in a myriad of Indian specialties. Try also: sautéing chicken briefly and then adding a little white wine and saffron and cooking until done; stirring a bit into mussels in garlicky broth; flavoring a sweet custard with saffron.*

# SAFFRON RICE WITH CASHEWS AND RAISINS

This rice is Indian inspired and so we call for traditional basmati, but Texmati rice will give much the same effect, and in fact any white rice is good made this way. Substitute almonds for the cashews if you prefer.

**SERVES 4**

1½ cups basmati rice

2¼ cups water

1 cinnamon stick, broken in half

5 cloves

2 bay leaves

¼ teaspoon crumbled saffron threads

1 teaspoon salt

2 tablespoons butter, softened

¼ cup chopped cashews

¼ cup raisins

Rinse the rice until the water runs clear. Put the rice in a medium saucepan with the water, cinnamon stick, cloves, bay leaves, saffron, and salt. Bring to a boil, reduce the heat to low, and cook, covered, for 15 minutes. Remove from the heat and let sit, without removing the lid, for 10 minutes. With a fork, gently stir in the butter, cashews, and raisins.

# MONKFISH COUSCOUS

Firm chunks of monkfish are ideal for simmering in a tomatoey broth flavored with garlic, saffron, cumin, and cayenne. Serve the fish over a mound of steaming couscous to soak up all the delicious liquid.

**WINE RECOMMENDATION**
No meek-spirited white wine for this fish! Choose a full-bodied white with earthy, as opposed to fruity, flavor. Candidates include white Rhône wines from France, southern Italian whites, such as Greco di Tufo, and even Greek whites.

**SERVES 4**

2 tablespoons cooking oil

1 onion, chopped

3 cloves garlic, chopped

About 3 cups water

3½ cups canned tomatoes (one 28-ounce can), drained and chopped, liquid reserved

1½ teaspoons salt

½ teaspoon ground cumin

¼ teaspoon fresh-ground black pepper

⅛ teaspoon cayenne

½ teaspoon packed saffron threads

1½ pounds monkfish fillets, membranes removed, fish cut into 1-inch pieces

3 tablespoons chopped fresh parsley

1⅓ cups couscous

1. In a large pot, heat the oil over moderately low heat. Add the onion and garlic and cook, stirring occasionally, until the onion is translucent, about 5 minutes.

2. Add enough water to the reserved tomato juice to equal 2 cups. Add this to the onion mixture along with the tomatoes, 1 teaspoon of the salt, the cumin, black pepper, and cayenne. Crumble in the saffron. Bring to a boil, reduce the heat, and simmer, covered, for 10 minutes.

3. Add the monkfish. Cook until the fish is just done, 3 to 4 minutes. Stir in 2 tablespoons of the parsley.

4. Meanwhile, in a medium saucepan, bring 2 cups of water and the remaining ½ teaspoon salt to a boil. Stir in the couscous. Cover, remove from the heat, and let sit for 5 minutes.

5. To serve, mound the couscous onto plates and top with the fish and vegetables. Ladle the liquid over the top and sprinkle with the remaining 1 tablespoon parsley.

**STAR ANISE** *Pretty star anise looks like an eight-petaled flower or, of course, a many-pointed star. And, yes, this dried fruit from a Chinese evergreen does taste like anise. The spice is used mainly in Chinese cuisine and in Thai and Vietnamese dishes that have a Chinese influence. In the West, it's more often found in infused syrups, and its oil flavors anisette liqueurs. You can buy star anise at Chinese markets and some supermarkets. It comes whole, broken, or ground; the first two are the better bets, since once ground, star anise loses flavor rapidly. Resist the temptation to add more and more star anise just because it's so attractive. Too much can be overly pungent.* ✽ **USES** *Star anise is one of the five spices in Chinese five-spice powder, along with Szechuan peppercorns, cinnamon, fennel seeds, and cloves. Long-simmered pork, duck, and chicken dishes often feature star anise, especially those including soy sauce. It's good with seafood, shellfish, and pumpkin, too. Try also: adding star anise to chicken noodle soup; steaming duck with it and then drying and wok-frying the duck until crisp; putting it in the poaching liquid for fish; dropping a few star anise into hot apple cider or mulled wine.*

# PLUM COMPOTE WITH STAR ANISE

Plums and star anise form a brilliant and novel pairing. Although you don't eat it, we like to leave the star anise in the syrup because it looks so beautiful; you can remove it if you prefer. Serve the compote with pound cake or butter cookies.

**SERVES 4**

1½  cups dry white wine

1½  cups water

½  cup sugar, more if the plums are tart

8  whole star anise

2  pounds red and/or black plums (about 9), halved and pitted

½  teaspoon lemon juice

1. In a medium stainless-steel saucepan, combine the wine, water, sugar, and star anise and bring to a simmer over moderately high heat.

2. Add the plums. Bring the poaching liquid back to a simmer and cook, partially covered, until the plums are just tender, 10 to 15 minutes. Pour the plums and their liquid into a glass or stainless-steel bowl and let cool. Stir in the lemon juice.

## VARIATIONS

■ You can use **red wine** instead of white.
■ Add several strips of **orange zest** to the saucepan along with the star anise.

# Chinese Poached Chicken Breasts with Star Anise

Chicken breasts poached in a broth flavored with star anise, cinnamon, ginger, scallions, and soy sauce is a Chinese classic. Traditionally you would save, not serve, the broth—it improves each time you use it—but we can never resist serving it with the chicken as a light sauce. If you like, boil noodles separately and add them to the broth for a meal in a dish.

**WINE RECOMMENDATION**
The exotic yet delicate broth requires a flavorful but light white wine. A German riesling would be ideal; if the riesling you choose has some slight sweetness, all the better.

**SERVES 4**

3½ cups canned low-sodium chicken broth or homemade stock

2 carrots, cut diagonally into ½-inch slices

6 scallions including green tops, 5 cut into 4-inch lengths, 1 chopped

6 ½-inch slices peeled fresh ginger, smashed, plus 2 tablespoons minced fresh ginger

4 cloves garlic, smashed

¼ cup brown sugar, preferably dark

¼ cup soy sauce

5 whole star anise

3 cinnamon sticks

6 black peppercorns

¼ teaspoon salt

¼ cup dry sherry

4 boneless, skinless chicken breasts (about 1⅓ pounds in all)

1. In a large saucepan, combine the broth, carrots, the 5 scallions, the smashed ginger, the garlic, brown sugar, soy sauce, star anise, cinnamon sticks, peppercorns, and salt. Bring to a boil, reduce the heat, and simmer, covered, for 20 minutes.

2. Add the sherry and chicken and bring back to a simmer over moderately low heat, covered. Turn the chicken and simmer, covered, until the chicken is just done, about 5 minutes.

3. With a slotted spoon, transfer the chicken, carrots, and star anise to large shallow bowls. Strain the broth and add the minced ginger and 2 tablespoons of the chopped scallion. Ladle the broth over the chicken and top with the remaining chopped scallion.

## TURMERIC

*Everything turmeric touches turns an intense yellow—in fact, the spice is in ballpark mustard primarily for that purpose—but turmeric has many other virtues. It brings a slightly bitter, musky taste to the table. It helps vegetables retain their color, keeping the greens green and the reds red. And it's one of the cheapest spices in the world. But don't let its yellowness and its low price tag tempt you to substitute turmeric for the much costlier saffron; although turmeric is sometimes called Indian saffron, the spices are not interchangeable. This boiled, dried, and then ground rhizome is almost always sold in powdered form. A small quantity is all you'll need.* ❊ **USES** *Turmeric lends its color to more than mustard; it also provides the yellow in commercial curry powder. The spice is often used with beans and lentils, rice, tomatoes, broccoli, and fish. Try also: including turmeric in Indian pilafs and dals as well as in braised vegetables, especially cauliflower; rubbing a chicken with turmeric and garlic before roasting; stirring a little into stir-fried shrimp and green onions and then adding a bit of lemon juice; making the English favorite kedgeree with rice, turmeric, cream, and smoked fish.*

# BROCCOLI WITH TURMERIC AND TOMATOES

Looking for a quick and easy way to add some excitement to broccoli? Both florets and stems lend their unique textures to this excellent side dish. We actually prefer the stems and hate to see them thrown away. Serve the broccoli with chicken, beef, or lamb.

**SERVES 4**

2   tablespoons cooking oil

2   onions, cut into thin slices

¾   teaspoon turmeric

1½  pounds broccoli (about 2 large stalks), stems peeled and cut crosswise into ¼-inch slices, tops cut into florets (about 7 cups in all)

1   cup drained canned diced tomatoes (from one 15-ounce can)

⅓   cup water

¾   teaspoon salt

1.  In a large, deep frying pan, heat the oil over moderate heat. Add the onions and cook, covered, stirring occasionally, for 5 minutes. Uncover and cook, stirring occasionally, until the onions are very soft, about 5 minutes longer.

2.  Stir in the turmeric to coat the onions. Stir in the broccoli, tomatoes, water, and salt and bring to a simmer. Reduce the heat and simmer, covered, until the broccoli is tender, about 10 minutes.

# CAULIFLOWER, POTATO, AND PEA CURRY

Our version of this curry, a favorite combination of vegetables in India, unites cumin, coriander, turmeric, and red-pepper flakes. Fresh cilantro provides an herbal note. Serve the curry as a generous side dish or with rice for a meatless main dish.

**WINE RECOMMENDATION**
Go for your favorite full-bodied, full-flavored white wine. A California chardonnay, for example, won't be wiped out by the curry's earthy and hot spices.

**SERVES 4**

- ¼ cup cooking oil
- 1 tablespoon ground coriander
- 1½ teaspoons ground cumin
- ½ teaspoon turmeric
- ¼ teaspoon dried red-pepper flakes
- 1 medium head cauliflower (about 1 pound), cut into large florets (about 4 cups)
- 1½ pounds boiling potatoes (about 4), peeled and cut into 1½-inch pieces
- 1 cup canned crushed tomatoes in thick puree
- ½ cup chopped cilantro
- ½ cup water
- 1 teaspoon salt
- 1 cup frozen petite peas

1. In a large deep frying pan, heat the oil over moderate heat. Add the coriander, cumin, turmeric, and red-pepper flakes and stir. Add the cauliflower and potatoes and cook, stirring frequently, until the vegetables start to soften, about 5 minutes.

2. Add the tomatoes, ¼ cup of the cilantro, the water, and the salt. Bring to a simmer, reduce the heat to low, and cook, covered, until the vegetables are tender, about 15 minutes. Stir in the peas and the remaining ¼ cup cilantro and cook, covered, until the peas are tender, about 2 minutes longer.

## VARIATION

If you like, you can add three tablespoons dried unsweetened **coconut** to the curry. Put it in at the same time as the peas.

# More about Herbs and Spices

Look to this section for practical help in combining herbs and spices with each other and with a wide variety of foods. You'll also find descriptions of unusual herbs and spices—and common substitutes for them.

RECIPES PICTURED OPPOSITE: (top) pages 159, 157, 171; (center) pages 67, 137, 59; (bottom) pages 71, 173, 87

# A Perfect Match

Certain foods have an affinity for particular herbs and spices. Although there are many other delicious combinations, we've listed some of our favorites here.

## Vegetables

| | |
|---|---|
| ARTICHOKES | bay leaves, parsley, oregano, thyme |
| BEETS | basil, dill, mint |
| BELL PEPPERS | basil, oregano, rosemary |
| BROCCOLI | red pepper, savory, turmeric |
| CABBAGE | caraway seeds, juniper berries |
| CARROTS | allspice, celery seeds, cumin, dill, marjoram, mint |
| CAULIFLOWER | chives, coriander, sage, turmeric |
| CORN | basil, chives, dill seeds, oregano |
| CUCUMBERS | dill, mint |
| EGGPLANT | basil, cumin |
| FENNEL | caraway seeds, fennel seeds, rosemary, thyme |
| GREEN BEANS | basil, dill, savory |
| MUSHROOMS | black pepper, marjoram, nutmeg, parsley, oregano, sage, tarragon, thyme |
| PEAS | mint, tarragon, turmeric |
| POTATOES | caraway seeds, chives, dill, dill seeds, paprika, parsley, thyme, turmeric |
| SPINACH | dill, nutmeg, tarragon |
| TOMATOES | basil, cilantro, cumin, dill, fennel seeds, oregano, red pepper, rosemary, saffron, tarragon, thyme |
| WINTER SQUASH | cinnamon, ginger, sage |
| ZUCCHINI | basil, oregano |

## Cheese, Eggs, Fish, Chicken, Meat, and Legumes

| | |
|---|---|
| CHEESE | chives, nutmeg, oregano, red pepper, sage, tarragon, thyme |
| EGGS | chives, parsley, tarragon |
| FISH | bay leaves, celery seeds, chives, dill, lemongrass, mint, mustard, paprika, parsley, red pepper, saffron, sage, tarragon, thyme |
| CHICKEN | basil, cilantro, cinnamon, lemongrass, marjoram, paprika, star anise, tarragon |
| BEEF | basil, black pepper, cumin, lemongrass, mustard, oregano |
| LAMB | cinnamon, cumin, marjoram, mint, rosemary, thyme |
| PORK | allspice, caraway seeds, celery seeds, coriander, juniper berries, mustard, paprika, sage |
| VEAL | dill, paprika, parsley |
| LEGUMES | basil, cumin, parsley, rosemary, sage, savory |

## Fruits

| | |
|---|---|
| APPLES | cardamom, cinnamon, cloves, ginger, nutmeg |
| BERRIES | black pepper, mint, star anise |
| CRANBERRIES | cloves, ginger |
| MANGOES | cilantro |
| ORANGES | cardamom, fennel seeds, mint, thyme |
| PEACHES | cloves, nutmeg |
| PEARS | bay leaves, black pepper, cardamom, cinnamon, star anise |
| PINEAPPLE | cloves, ginger, lemongrass, mint, rosemary |
| PLUMS | cinnamon, cloves, nutmeg, star anise |

# HERB AND SPICE COMBINATIONS

Supermarket shelves are lined with herb and spice mixtures for every occasion. These blends are convenient, but it's good to know the ingredients in traditional combinations in case you want to mix your own. You can then adjust the proportions to suit your own palate. Our list of basics includes a couple of classic fresh-herb combinations, too.

## HERBS

### Bouquet Garni
Used to flavor stocks, soups, and stews, a bouquet garni is simply a few sprigs of parsley, a sprig of thyme, and a bay leaf tied together with kitchen string. You can tie them around a piece of celery or inside a pouch of cheesecloth, if you like, or poke them into a tea ball. Drop the bouquet garni into your soup or stew and tie the other end of the string around a handle of the pot. When the soup's done, fish the bundle out and discard it. This is a great place to use parsley's flavorful stems.

### Fines Herbes
Chop equal parts fresh chervil, parsley, tarragon, and chives for the classic herb combination fines herbes. Part of its charm is its delicacy and freshness, retained by adding the mixture to a dish at the last minute. Dried herbs just wouldn't have the same effect. Sprinkle a handful of fines herbes over pasta tossed with olive oil, an omelet, or a vegetable sauté. Or mix the herbs with softened butter to top sautéed fish, chicken, or steak.

### Herbes de Provence
The famous dried herb mixture from southern France, herbes de Provence, can include thyme, savory, rosemary, marjoram, sage, lavender, bay leaves, basil, and despite the name *herbes*, fennel seeds—which are actually a spice. In commercial preparations, the particular ingredients and their proportions vary tremendously by brand. To make your own, combine the ingredients according to your taste and use the mixture with braised lamb or chicken or in a stew of Provençal vegetables.

# SPICES

### Chili Powder
Commercial chili-powders include paprika, cayenne, black pepper, salt, cumin, oregano, garlic powder, and occasionally coriander and cloves. Make your own mix without the salt or garlic powder; add fresh garlic to the dish during cooking and season with salt to taste.

### Curry Powder
A blend of many spices goes into commercial curry powder. You may find cayenne, cinnamon, coriander, cloves, cumin, fennel seeds, fenugreek, ground mustard, black pepper, turmeric, and more. The telltale yellow color comes from the turmeric, and the heat level ranges from mild to spicy; hotter blends are generally labeled Madras. If you've ever tasted one of the remarkable curries of India, though, you'll know that Indian cooks don't use prepared powder. There, individual spices are toasted, ground, and combined in amounts suitable to a particular dish. Since many of the spices involved are quite strong, you may want to start off your personalized blend with an easy combination of cumin and coriander, add a little cayenne if you're looking for heat, and work from there. If you do choose to use commercial powder, you can improve the flavor of those raw spices by sautéing them in a dry pan.

### Five-Spice Powder
Also called Chinese five-spice powder, this combination teams ground Szechuan peppercorns, cloves, cinnamon, fennel seeds, and star anise. The blend tastes great on pork and chicken and in Asian soups and noodle dishes. It's especially good with grated orange zest in vegetable stir-fries.

### Garam Masala
Another Indian spice blend, *garam masala* is a mixture of "warm" spices. The most traditional version combines cinnamon, cloves, cardamom, and black peppercorns, but newer variations can also include coriander, cumin, and mace or nutmeg. *Garam masala* is generally added at the end of cooking so that the enticing aroma remains strong when the dish is served.

### Quatre-Épices
The French four-spice mixture, *quatre-épices*, is made up of ground pepper, nutmeg, cloves, and ginger (or cinnamon). It's traditionally used to season sausages, stews, and pâtés, and adds an interesting kick to fruit desserts, too.

# Unusual Herbs and Spices

You probably don't use these herbs and spices in your everyday cooking but may run across them in recipes. For descriptions and suggested substitutes, check below.

**Ajowan**  Though greenish-brown striped ajowan seeds look similar to cumin or caraway seeds, they taste more like thyme. They're hot and slightly bitter, so add them sparingly. Use ajowan whole or ground in Indian cooking or with beans and other legumes to aid digestion. **SUBSTITUTE:** *Dried thyme*

**Annatto**  Also known as achiote, annatto is valued as much for its color as its flavor; in fact, in very small quantities, the spice is virtually flavorless and is used as a dye for cheeses and margarine. In larger amounts, it lends a peppery spiciness as well as a distinctive reddish-yellow color to rice, vegetable dishes, and stews. To intensify the hue, heat the seeds in oil. **SUBSTITUTE:** *Turmeric and black pepper*

**Asafetida**  Actually a resin, asafetida comes in a brown chunk or a tan-colored powder and is a spice to use in tiny quantities. In powdered form, it has a terrible scent, which disappears when the spice is cooked; it then imparts an onionlike aroma. Use asafetida in Indian, Middle Eastern, and vegetable cooking. **SUBSTITUTE:** *Scallions or onions*

**Borage**  Every bit of borage tastes like cucumber—the stems, the fuzzy greenish-gray leaves, even the bright-blue flowers. Borage adds flavor to drinks (like Pimm's Cup) and salads. **SUBSTITUTE:** *Slices of cucumber*

**Chervil**  Lacy chervil leaves, from one of the most delicate herbs around, carry a mild anise flavor. This member of the fines herbes quartet should be used fresh; the dried herb has little flavor. Add it just before serving. **SUBSTITUTE:** *Tarragon*

**Curry Leaves**  A component of some curry powders, these small, shiny green leaves come from the curry plant. They have a citrusy scent, similar to that of lemongrass, and a pungent bittersweet flavor. The herb is used in Indian curries and vegetable dishes, often sautéed separately in oil and then stirred in at the last moment to accentuate the aroma. **SUBSTITUTE:** *Lemon zest*

**Epazote**  Used often in the Mexican kitchen, epazote has a strong odor and a pungent, pleasantly bitter flavor. Simmer it with dried beans or other starchy dishes. The herb, found in Mexican and Latin markets, dries well. **SUBSTITUTE:** *Oregano*

**Fenugreek**  Brown fenugreek seeds are both bitter and sweet, with a mild celery flavor. Lightly toasting them removes some of the bitterness, but be sure not to burn them or they'll be even more bitter. Fenugreek is available in seed form or ground and is a common ingredient in commercial curry powder. Use it in moderation to flavor vegetables and legumes. **SUBSTITUTE:** *Lovage or fresh celery leaves*

**Lavender**  Use lavender's greenish-gray leaves and violet flowers either fresh or dried. Lavender is often an ingredient in herbes de Provence, and its eucalyptus flavor is delicious in tisanes, ice cream, candies, and with beef and lamb. **SUBSTITUTE:** *Cardamom*

**Lemon Balm**  The wrinkled green leaves of lemon balm look like mint but have a fresh lemony flavor. Add them to tea (warm or iced) or fruit salad, or to fish or chicken dishes toward the end of cooking time. Although dried leaves are good for tea in the wintertime, fresh leaves are best. **SUBSTITUTE:** *Lemongrass, lemon zest*

**Lemon Verbena**  Of all the lemony herbs, lemon verbena has the strongest lemon scent. Its flavor is strong, too, so use it sparingly in tea, fruit drinks, salads, and any place you'd like a citrus flavor. Lemon verbena dries well and can be used for a straight tisane or brewed along with black tea. **SUBSTITUTE:** *Lemongrass, lemon zest*

**Lovage**  Lovage's dark-green leaves are packed with celery flavor but have a distinctive spiciness all their own. You can use the leaves, stems, and roots of this herb; the strong flavor works well in stuffings, soups, and stews. **SUBSTITUTE:** *Fresh celery leaves*

**Shiso Leaves**  Dark green (or red) shiso leaves have a distinctive flavor, vaguely reminiscent of mint. They're used in Japanese cooking, in soups, noodle dishes, tempura, and even sushi, and can be found in Asian markets. **SUBSTITUTE:** *Basil or mint leaves*

# INDEX

Page numbers in **boldface** indicate photographs ❦ indicates wine recommendations
🌿 indicates recipes featuring that herb ❦ indicates recipes featuring that spice

## Q

## R

## S